AUTHOR BIOGRAPHY

Born and raised initially in Brighton, then around Europe before returning to the United Kingdom, my childhood was unusual to say the least. There was a 42 year gulf of ages between my parents who met during their stage careers, father being the show owner, mother one of the dancers – their relationship was tempestuous to say the least. My father was the better carer of the two, he was 67 when he fathered me, but I remember him doing his best to look after myself and my two sisters.

During one point when I was about two or three years old, my mother had taken us to stay with relatives and in one of his letters he described me as being '90% bullheaded mule'. I often wonder what I had done to deserve this accolade. As father was about 6ft 2ins, and me a small squit of a girl – I obviously had learned to stand my ground against a giant foe. I am ever grateful to have been taught to look after myself by a legend of a man.

My mother and father split when I was six, by the time I was 16 I had moved house 18 times, country four times, and had attended 14 different schools. I left school at 14 to work with a wood carver, to be returned to school when we came back to England at the age of 15.

The disjointed nomadic travels of mother and step-father, together with the genetic makeup of East End Londoner, mixed with a Texan Cowboy of Scottish and Mexican ancestry, I could not hope to ever be 'normal'.

CW01496264

1

CC Readers – Publishing
61 Bridge Street, Kington, Herefordshire, HR5 3DJ
enquiries@ccreaders.co.uk

ISBN: 9798812419127

*To Petra
with love*

This book is dedicated to
Christopher E. Howard,
The Author of 'Excalibur – *Found!'*
and 'Ghost, Be Mine!'
amongst many others.

Chris encouraged me to follow my dreams,
he inspired me to finish this book
which I initially started in 1984.

*One of the loveliest
Ladies I have
worked with,
and an honour
to call her
friend.

from Cordelia.
xxx
xx
x*

III

Manners, Morals and Motorbikes
by
C J McLeod

MANNERS, MORALS AND MOTORBIKES

PHEW......!

MANNERS, MORALS AND MOTORBIKES

FOREWORD

Over the years many people have asked me the same questions: Whatever made you start riding motorcycles? Did your father, uncles or brothers inspire your love of motorbikes? Did you have a boyfriend who left you his motorcycle as a split-up settlement?

The straightforward answer was that I simply wanted to be independent. I didn't seem to be able to drive a car, and to get a bike on the road didn't firstly necessitate any form of driving test. It was that easy.

The thrill of actually owning my own motorcycle was just so complete, that I have never since considered not having my own. I hope that whoever reads this book, if not smitten with a desire to follow suit, will not openly adversely pre-judge someone on the sole basis that they appear on one of these joyous machines. I also want to share some of the funnier moments which most motorcycle riders have in common, as many of the anecdotal passages in this book happen time and time again. Also, I hope to give much food for thought against the social trend to outcast any person who appears to have views and ideas which differ from the general rule.

We are all individuals, and we ought to be allowed to have our own standards. The only overall rule ought to be to 'LIVE AND LET LIVE', so long as your personal enjoyment is not detrimental to anyone else's ability to enjoy their own life, then it ought to be an acceptable pastime.

LIVE, LOVE, LOSE, LEARN AND LAUGH.

Chapter 1

THE DAWN OF INDEPENDENCE

Living in a country area made teenage life difficult. In small villages there was not very much to do during the evenings, the only excitement was when there was a dance at one of the larger towns in the area. I was first invited to one of these dances by a schoolfriend when I was fifteen years old. The dance hall had laid on a courtesy bus from the surrounding villages, including ours, leaving from the village green at half past seven, to arrive at the dance hall at about eight o'clock. We were then to meet the return bus at quarter to midnight in order to get home.

The freedom of not having to get mum or dad to taxi us out was great, and my friend Janice and I soon got into a regular routine, mostly going to the Pavilion on a Friday night, and the Lynx on a Saturday night. Many nights of innocent enjoyment commenced. It was a lovely carefree time, most of the local bands played a lot of rock and roll, although many types of music were played. The important thing being that it was danceable.

These local hops produced many hours of pleasure which did not only cover the weekend evenings, but also the weekday evenings too, as the pair of us tried to learn some of the dances that the girls were doing. We met many other girls and boys and the flirtations were fun and innocent.

Sometimes, the dance halls would manage to get some bigger names to come and play at the venues, greatly increasing our excitement and pleasure. However, the problems then started as some of the larger bands who we obviously wanted to watch, would arrive late, sometimes not starting to play until half past eleven or even later. This meant that if we were to see our favourite groups then we would have to miss the bus home, and get alternative transport arranged. Our parents could not understand why it was so important to see these bands when we could see them on the telly on 'Top of the Pops', or listen to them on the radio. They could not understand why they should turn out late at night when there were perfectly good courtesy buses laid on.

In the early seventies the only other alternative transport was if we knew anyone in the village who had their own car. In those days that invariably meant one of the lads, as girls just didn't drive. This did not cause too much hassle as we always put some money towards the petrol, although as we got older and more shapely things started getting out of hand. A couple of the lads would hope to get more than just a thank you, and it became a bit of a game to them to offer a lift home but take us to a nearby lover's lane to try their luck, and hopefully get a grope or two into the bargain. We prepared ourselves for this though. I had a dog at the time, and Janice and I used to go on walks to the woods most days, until we knew exactly where we were at any spot in the area. As the dance halls were approximately ten miles away, we decided that the lover's lane being only about one or two miles away, it was at least closer to home. Many was the lad who unwittingly lost out in this way. When they drove us to the car park, and started trying it on, we would perhaps give a little cuddle, or even a kiss or two if we felt like it, we would then ask to be taken home.

If the lads were more persistent or pushy, then as soon as we had had enough we would make an excuse to get out of the car, sometimes on the pretext of needing a pee, sometimes because it was such a lovely evening and it would be more comfortable to have a bit more room to move. The end results were, we would nip home along the tracks, leaving the boys to look for us, thinking they had frightened us. Once they realised that a ride for a ride was not our game, they had the choice to have a contribution towards petrol costs or find someone more playful.

Very few lads minded this treatment as it was always done in a friendly manner, and although a laugh was had by all, we would always speak afterwards on their level, making it clear that what we said was what we meant. Once the ground rules were established, we soon worked out which lads were not worth asking.

When we got home, my mum was very lenient (as often as not she was still out on the tiles herself) and it was mostly open house so we often invited our friends in for cups of coffee. This was alright most of the time, although one of the boys got quite a shock one night. My friend Janice always had to get back quickly so after she was dropped off one night, John drove me on home and came in for a coffee. We were sitting at the dining room table, quite happily drinking our drinks and putting the world to rights. The bottom half of the window was open (an old sash window) as it was a lovely night and the cool air was refreshing after the stuffy smokiness of the dance hall.

I sat with my back to the hallway door and heard my stepfather call out. He opened the door, and as he entered the room I was astonished to see John jump up and dive out of the window in a blind panic, yelling and screaming as he went. I turned around to see my stepfather holding a shotgun in his hands. Poor John! My stepfather was a shooting enthusiast, and having a bit of arthritis he found it difficult to open this particular gun up for cleaning. He had wanted John to help open the gun for him. I had a lot of apologizing to do the next day when I caught up with John, but we had a good laugh out of his sudden exit. He even came back home and helped my stepfather with cleaning his guns, as it turned out to be one of his hobbies too.

After a while we had a large group of friends, and we would often meet up during the days; it was nice to belong to such a friendly group of people. We would always have plenty to talk about, and do. One warm summer evening, having nothing better to do, we went up to the local railway yard which was disused and totally disconnected from the main line. We were obviously not meant to be there, but the sense of being somewhere out of bounds greatly enhanced the excitement and fun of the occasion. This particular night, joy of joys, we struck gold. There was one of those old line maintenance platforms like they show in the movies. An old pump action platform that you had to pump manually in order to make it move up and down the railway track which was still in situ. There was about ten of us, three of us on each pump handle, and two hanging each side, trying to keep a precarious balance without getting clobbered on the head by the pump bars as they were worked up and down. The pump would get up steam and roll faster and faster, and sometimes be more difficult to stop than it was to start it. Luckily when we got going we had about five miles of country track to practice on. Having found this great pastime, we went there for several evenings over the next few weeks. We had to be as quiet as possible because the local police station backed onto this bit of track, about 800 yards from the railway yard, but once clear of that and the houses for the next half mile, this great danger behind us, we were able to really go for it, we were off. Laughing and singing along the way, we did not feel we were doing any harm and were actually quite mindful of the dangers of the machine and were as careful as possible. Our favourite spot was the old bridge over the main road, about two miles from home, we would get there and stop short of the bridge, leaving the platform in the cover of some shrubs and bushes, sitting there chatting and passing the time away.

Unfortunately, this era in our life came to an abrupt halt when one of our friends, who had a relative in the police force, told us that the police were out to get us. We did not wish to give in easily, so we stole away with our prized trolley once more, but on the way home as we approached the police station, one of the girls got into a nervous coughing fit, another one got a fit of giggles, and one of the lads thought he saw a glimmer of light further up the track and there was a sudden noise. With hindsight the noise was probably a car backfiring, but that was enough, we all jumped off the trolley in a mad scramble, falling on top of each other, leaving the trolley in full flight to run on and crash into the railway yard unattended. We picked ourselves up and took off over the fields as though our lives depended on it. We dispersed for that night, and had endless fun discussing the event, and whether anyone had been caught or not, but on a headcount during the next few evenings we concluded that no-one had been apprehended. However, next time we went to go out on our platform, we found that it had had its wheels taken off, so ended that particular pastime.

It was a heady time to be young, and, tinged with the danger of being discovered doing wrong gave us a buzz. What a shame that youngsters of today are so stifled that the only escapes from society seem to be drink, or getting a high from the many harmful substances which are advertised to them. At least our kicks, although not totally without risk, were easy to recover from. The worst embarrassment was for our parents to hear that we were getting up to mischief. There would always be some adult ready to complain at our antics, although in our own way we tried not to directly affect anyone else's space, in the same way that we would have liked our own space respected. I still feel that adults interfere too much in the teenagers' lives. If you shield people too much, they never develop their own set of values, and it is too much to expect anyone to follow other's rules blindly. You only learn from your own mistakes, never from other's.

As time wore on, I realised that my mother could drive a car. If she could, I thought, why don't I learn? I asked her if she would find out how I could learn for myself. She said that she would try and teach me; if we could find somewhere to go off-road first. Good thinking. I asked some of the boys who could drive how and where had they learnt. Most of them had fathers who had taught them, some of the lads from the surrounding farms had been driving tractors on the fields first, and others had had proper lessons with driving instructors. On further investigation, I realised that I would not be able to afford proper lessons, but that it was quite common for a local airfield to be used for practice, so after sorting out the insurances needed for me, off we went.

The first time out we couldn't even find the airfield. However, after some discussion with some of her friends down the pub, we struck rich and arrived for my first lesson. After some disastrous attempts, I managed to get some idea of what I was doing, even to the extent of trying some reversing which mum emphasized was as important as going forwards if I was to learn to park without too much trouble. We should have carried on quietly from there, but no, my mum liked the occasional drink or ten, so we went to the pub on our way home to celebrate my first reasonably successful lesson.

Mistake!

Mum ended up having a few too many and was a bit worse for wear by the end of the night. Between us, we thought maybe I could drive home as I was at least sober. Confronted by the realisation that this was it, I was now in control of a missile, my nerves went to pieces. I managed to get started, then into gear and we bounced off into the great wide world of narrow roads, other traffic and loads of obstacles; my downfall was the obstacles; in the shape of a large wooden fence beside the railway bridge which seemed to attract the car as though it were magnetic. During the ensuing demolition process, I found the brakes of the car only just in time to stop, thankfully before the 15ft drop onto the old railway line. Mum rethought our strategy and decided that was enough. She took up her position behind the steering wheel and relieved me of duty. That was the end of her instructions (she sobered up at phenomenal speed), now I would have to save up for proper driving lessons as her nerves reasserted themselves. There was no way I could afford to run a car of my own even if I passed my car test, and by now I doubted if that would ever happen anyway. Maybe my destiny lay elsewhere.

Chapter 2

MY FIRST LESSONS IN MOTORCYCLING

Salvation came to me shortly after this episode in my life. A few weeks later, during a particularly pleasant Sunday afternoon, several of the gang met up. As we chatted and basked in the glorious weather, one of the boy's older brother turned up on a motorbike. We all admired the bike and had a sit on it. I thought that it looked like fun and noted the large red 'L' plates, front and back. I asked him why he didn't have to have someone with him. What luck, all you had to have was a learner driving licence, tax and insurance and hey presto, you were away. This was serious food for thought. I then singled out a few of the older lads for my attention, I wanted to have a ride on a bike to see if I liked it. Once I achieved a pillion ride I was hooked. The thrill was incredible, and the feeling of complete freedom was brilliant. I had to have one.

The first obstacle to this ambition was again learning to handle one of these marvelous machines, and who was gullible enough to teach me. Obviously mum couldn't, and probably wouldn't if she could. I didn't even know whether she would approve or not but that would come later. The less said the better. I cast around amongst the boys for a would-be tutor but most just laughed and said this was men's territory, women couldn't ride a bike properly and they certainly were not going to trust a girl with their precious machines. I got a lot of ribbing from the boys, all said I couldn't do it even if I tried, and with the recent memories of the driving skills to remind me, I even doubted myself. There were no official motorcycle schools I could turn to and I was beginning to feel despondent. Maybe it was an impossible dream as well.

Not long afterwards, attracted by their motorcycles, I met a different group of boys, and just had to try my luck again. This time it succeeded, but the reason for my success soon became apparent. I happened to ask the one lad who, unbeknown to me, had started dabbling in the odd smoke of grass and I had caught him during one of his lightheaded moments. A group of us had gone up to the woods where there was a large clearing, and lots of wide tracks round and about the area. To me it was ideal as it was out of the way and I didn't think I could do much damage here. The lads were all laughing and joking and thought it would be a great laugh to see me make a fool of myself and were all for it. However, James was serious enough to actually try to tell me about all the different controls and what they were for. He sat on the bike and showed me how to pull away, balancing the throttle with the clutch release. The front brake was on the right-hand handlebar, the clutch on the left. So far so good. Now it started to get a bit more complicated. The throttle was on the right-hand bar too, making your hands have to work separately to your fingers. James dismounted and let me sit on the bike and feel the controls.

Now was the time, replace words with actions, start the engine. Being a gentleman James kickstarted the bike for me and ran beside me so that he was able to grab the brakes or handlebars if necessary. This all seemed easy enough. Yep. I was ready after a few practice stop and starts. Poor James valiantly got on the pillion seat and off we went. I jolted him backwards and forwards, forwards and back, by the time I got going his brains were fairly shook up, but I was enjoying myself immensely. I wasn't confident enough to lean around the bends yet but there was plenty of straight track to start. After a while I felt I had the hang of this and decided to try to turn around in a largish clearing. Whilst turning I got the controls out of balance again, spun the back wheel and in my panic I opened the throttle up fully. In this state of alarm the front end went light and inadvertently I lurched forward and rode up the trunk of a fallen tree in spectacular stunt ride fashion. Luckily I managed to remember the brakes and as we stopped dead, I stalled the machine; about ten feet up the trunk into its canopy. As we toppled sidewards, the branches broke our fall and caught us, slowing our descent, the bike heavier than we were broke through to the ground first, with us sliding into a heap on top of it. Although suffering several scratches our clothing had saved the biggest part of us, and the bike survived without major damage. James was a gibbering mess, but in his elevated state of consciousness said that it was like riding a horse, if you don't fall sometimes, you don't learn to ride properly. He made me ride back to the others, bless him. I owe him a lot.

Mind you. He declined the offer of another tuition stint and volunteered his mate for the next round. This went a lot better, and after about another twenty minutes I was again quite confident. I was by now truly inspired, and when Pete had had enough I pestered until James said that I was good enough to go by myself for a little while, as they wanted to relax in the sunshine. I didn't need telling twice, so off I went, happy as a little sandgirl.

Pride usually goes before a fall, and sure enough it happened. I was quite happily riding about down the track and enjoying my newfound skills to the full. However, when I reached the bottom of a fairly large dip, quite a way from the lads, the bike stopped inexplicably. I tried for all I was worth, first to kickstart it, then to push the bike back to the clearing, but I did not have the power to get the bike back up the hill. After trying for about 10 minutes I decided that it was too much and the boys would have to come and get both me and the machine. The motorbike was not particularly big, being a 175cc twin cylinder machine, but as I was only a small framed adolescent girl, inexperienced to boot, it seemed too heavy and I was tired by this time. I thought I would sit down for a minute and rest before going back to get the boys to help. Feeling pleased about the progress I had made so far this afternoon; I lay back in the sunshine and closed my eyes. Then I fell asleep.

After I had been gone for about an hour, the boys started getting worried and came looking for me. They called out, but I couldn't hear them as I was sound asleep. They had been chatting and laughing as per usual, and hadn't even noticed what direction I had gone, but now they were worried. James by this time had confessed about the incident with the tree and they were really frightened that I was in dire straits. It took them about another thirty-five minutes before they found me, and then they nearly died. From the top of the dip, all they could see was the bike abandoned on its side where I had dumped it, and me a little way away lying totally still. Dave fell head over heels in his hurry to get down to me, and twisted his ankle, the others just scrabbled down the dip as fast as they could go. They were all really angry with me when I woke up and said I had just fallen asleep. James thought I had crashed his bike and at first wouldn't believe me when I said it had just packed up for no reason. He said it wouldn't just pack up like that as he looked after it, meticulously. Tempers flew on all sides as the boys tried to mend the bike, until it dawned on us all that it had run out of petrol, which is why I could not re-start it. They were still angry that I hadn't just come to get them, and they refused to let me ride it anymore.

Nothing daunted, I set about getting a bit more experience as and when I could. It was not easy to talk someone round after the first session leaked out amongst the fellas, although after a few weeks even James grudgingly admitted that I had managed better than he had expected, especially after taking him up the tree which in hindsight gave us the giggles. James was surprised to see me still try to ride after that one, as he admitted that he had been scared silly. I talked him into another lesson, but this time on the old airfield and as this was just the two of us it went a lot better. This effort was not without incident though, poor James had never known that a bike could 'kangaroo' for so long, (about 400 yards) but I had the bug and nothing was going to stop me now.

For the next few months I badgered all the lads to let me have a go on their various motorbikes. Some were really sporting, others were very derisory, telling me to leave the piloting to them as that was their domain. I was having none of that though, and I still don't see why men should have all the fun.

One of the lads called Kevin had a really nice motorcycle and sidecar. That looked quite a challenge and I hoped that he might let me have a go. I started dating with Kevin as I really fancied him too, but I should have known better than to mix business with pleasure. Although this motorbike was a lot larger engine size, it seemed it might be easier to handle than a solo machine, as I wouldn't have to worry about keeping my balance, but if anyone out there has ever ridden a combination as they are commonly called, they will know that that assumption was just another big mistake. There is no way that a bike and sidecar is easy. Kevin tried his best to put me off, telling me of all the various reasons why it wasn't as easy as it looked. As this didn't deter me one bit, he said that if I could start the bike he would let me have a go. He showed me how this was done, explaining how to set it up with all the different levers which were on the handlebars. There was a decompressor and an advance/retard lever, both were to do with lowering the pressure in the engine to somehow make it easier to start. Or so he said! Then you had to play with the kickstarter and try to feel the engine as it got near the power stroke, the kickstarter would go stiffer, the kickstart was then to be freed off and it was all set for the big kick. As the bike was a large 500cc single cylinder this was the hard part.

I weighed in at less than eight stone, and no matter how hard I tried, I could not swing the kickstart down as shown. I ended up standing on the kickstart on one leg, holding on to the handlebars, my body at a parallel to the ground looking as though I were doing some sort of touch my toes routine, combined with a balancing act. Kevin looked alarmed at my determination not to be outsmarted and told me not to try as I might hurt myself. This had the usual opposite effect, I jumped on the blasted kickstart with all my might. The ensuing flight was not what I had expected at all. The kickstart lever swung down with my landing, and with a massive backfire, kicked back so hard that I flew over the handlebars and landed about a meter in front of the machine. Mistaking my stupidity for guts, Kevin succumbed to my desire and started the machine for me, he let me loose, with him able to supervise from the chair.

A sidecar is unlike any other roadgoing machinery in that it does not drive equally around corners. If going around a left hand bend, the motorbike has to overtake the sidecar and one has to open up the power, using body weight if possible to help steer and thence go round the bend. When negotiating a right hand bend the reverse has to happen, and the motorcycle has to go slower, (brake) in order to let the sidecar drift around the motorbike. This is because there is only power driving the rear motorcycle wheel, and the sidecar is effectively dead weight. This was not explained to me, and I did not appreciate this particular difficulty. Hence, although the more undulating bends thereto had not caused me much grief, I promptly got everything all crossed up at a tight right-handed railway bridge.

I hit the wall of the bridge fairly hard with the sidecar, the jolt swung the motorcycle round, stopping with a thud against the wall, throwing me up and over the handlebars once more. I ended up peering over the edge of the bridge wall. It took me less than ten minutes to demolish the sidecar portion and after the breakages were inspected, we had to unhitch the chair and leave it as a solo machine. I honestly don't know to this day what made me carry on wanting to learn to ride, but I was undaunted and this incident helped form the decision that I was safer on a machine which was only my width, as I didn't have to think much more than whether I would get through a gap myself. I definitely could not cope with anything wider than about two feet. Just as well, as the sidecar had just been rendered useless. My newfound romance suffered a similar fate, although we did remain friends for a long time afterwards. Apparently I was just too wild and woolly for him to cope with, even though he did admit I was great fun. He just wanted to have some sort of ego and pride left. Bless him.

Soon after this last incident, I got another opportunity to practice my riding off-road. There was a group of bikers living in a nearby village where they were able to use an old railway junction area. This was after the massive governmental de-railing scheme during the mid-nineteen sixties. The junction had been one of the largest railway stations in the country, almost rivalling Clapham Junction in size. All that now remained was about 55 acres of rough wasteland. It was quite common practice for the lads to get their bikes out and play around on their free days. I happened to go there with a group of mates and their machines, and it was not long before I had fully entered into the spirit of events. Sure enough, I got hold of a motorcycle and off I went. It was okay for the first few minutes, but within about fifteen minutes disaster struck. Namely me again.

What happened this time was that I was happily riding around on the motorbike when I got stuck in a deep rut. I could not get out of it, and another of the lads was heading towards me from behind, riding a bit quicker than I was. Trying to give me a fright, he came just a bit too close as he overtook me, and took me by surprise. I was spooked and wobbled – then CRASH. We hit each other side on. The bikes became entangled and stuck together, locking handlebar to handlebar, footrests to footrests. This meant:-

1. my throttle stuck open by his clutch
2. his clutch was stuck out by my throttle
3. my front brake stuck out past his clutch lever
4. my gear lever mangled together with his rear brake

my bike was dragging his, and I could not brake or get out of gear. He did not have enough brake power to stop both bikes. Neither of us were able to regain control as no controls were controllable. This left us riding off into the distance locked together in mortal combat. Fighting each other, blaming each other and trying to smack hell out of each other. Everyone else just collapsed with laughter, unable to either help or even stand up. We hit the hedge, crashed through it which helped slow us down, the ploughed field eventually brought us to a stop by bumping us about until we fell apart. Finally our mates came and helped us back to the wasteland, but not before the farmer had come out and mugged us for money to pay for the crops we had supposedly damaged.

Once we had gathered ourselves in, we were thankful that no-one had been hurt, the topic was milked for every last ounce of humour, and I was the butt for most of the more macho jokes as being female, 'I shouldn't have been there', although I am sure none of those present would have willingly missed the occasion and were quite happy to have someone to take the mickey out of. I didn't mind, because I felt that at last I was being taken seriously by the lads, and from then on I was accepted within their circles as an individual in my own right.

Chapter 3

GUESS WHAT I BOUGHT TONIGHT, MUM?

Having had my share of problems at school due to an unusual and nomadic upbringing, I left at the age of 16. My first job was just seasonal, working in a pier-side Bingo arcade. This was quite fun and just what I needed to get the cobwebs out of my system. The work was a doddle, and I spent many hours of fun, talking to the holidaymakers, playing with the kids and forgetting about responsibilities altogether. This was a time for just being me, I owed no-one anything, and no-one owed me. Life was relatively carefree and great. Summer was to be enjoyed, and to be paid to work on the beach was freedom of the extreme. I was fairly well paid, and if we did well, our boss gave us a generous bonus. At first, most of my money went on clothes and trinkets, some towards my keep at home, and some just to spend. I soon realised though, that however much I wanted a motorbike I would have to save up for it myself, especially seeing that I still hadn't plucked up the courage to tell my parents that I was often riding as a pillion on friends bikes, let alone wanting one of my own.

I was very unsure of how to tackle that particular piece of information, but knowing that if it was not approved of, it would be more uncomfortable to have to lie rather than just not mention it. I never saw it as being a lie if the subject didn't crop up, although I did realise that it was only fair that my parents should know what I was up to. How I managed to avoid the actual issue I cannot imagine, but I was always one to just get on with my life with as little effect on others as possible. Even now, although I can be extremely explosive when upset, I am usually fairly unruffled and unemotional in my relationships. The hidden undercurrent is extremely stubborn and I knew that whatever my parents would say, I would still do what I wanted. I was never really openly defiant, but just got on with what I wanted to do, even so it still bothered me on how to deal with telling them with as little fuss as possible. Playing safe, I decided to wait until the subject came up.

During the summer I saved what monies I could and by September I had the grand sum of sixty-five pounds. I started looking at motorcycle magazines and scanning their classified sections to see what a motorbike would cost me. As I would be allowed to ride up to a 250cc machine when I was 17, I decided to keep saving until then as a machine would cost me in the region of two hundred pounds anyway. I lost my job at the end of the season, and looking around there was not much work to be had. I applied for a couple of vacancies and struck lucky at a local department store. I was taken on as a switchboard operator, with the chance of learning general office work if I was considered suitable. I enjoyed this work very much, and it didn't take me long to master the old plug and lead switchboard. The experience was great, and although to start with I often made some awful mistakes: cutting calls off by accident was quite easy, my optimistic outlook stood me in good stead, and I could usually talk my way out of trouble for the worst of my accidents.

One of the other girls in the office used to go to the dances as well, and we became great friends. Although we used to have a slightly different group of mates, we had similar interests and both of us had motorcycling boyfriends. She had been dating her particular boyfriend, Jeff, for some eighteen months and was supposed to be engaged to him. Karen lived about six miles in the opposite direction from my village, but her boyfriend lived in the village next to my man of the moment. I knew of him as he would drink in the same pub as my boyfriend during the week, and as I would go to their pub on the Wednesday night, I had already met him, although he was with another girl on those occasions. I let the cat out of the bag before I realised that he was supposed to be engaged to Karen.

Understandably Karen was extremely angry at being double crossed and she decided to get her own back before dumping him. I had already unwittingly told her a lot about the other girl so for a couple of weeks we played him along, not letting on that we worked together or even knew each other. She was quite merciless in winding him up by casually mentioning having met a certain girl from his area called Sara. It was quite funny to see him writhe about, trying to find out if she suspected anything had been going on or not. His eyes were bulging as she kept asking him if he knew her, or her boyfriend as she called him by a local nickname.

Karen and I decided to meet up at the dance at the weekend and spill the beans. Jeff was decidedly uncomfortable when I casually waved him in recognition, and proceeded to walk over and introduce myself to his friend (my friend Karen) and apparently innocently joined in his conversation with her. As he knew that I knew his other girlfriend, he kept trying to get rid of me by saying that so and so was here, and he thought they were at the other bar if I wanted to see them. Karen and my pre-arranged plans were much more entertaining for us, and we enjoyed his discomfiture to the full.

Between us we stage managed most of the conversation, without asking too directly who we were and so avoiding the actual necessity to mention the other girl's existence quite well. I had a laugh during the following Wednesday night's appearance at his local pub when he was with the other girl. I managed to go to the ladies' room at the same times as she did, and you could see the agony on his face when we came out, as he worried about whether I had said anything to her about Karen. We got two weeks' worth of entertainment at his expense before she gave him the elbow and told him exactly what she thought of his two-timing ways. As we were careful not to be seen chatting together for the next few months, he was left wondering how on earth Karen had found out about him, but we never let on. Why let him know how women know these things, better to let him think we were mysterious.

My pay at the office was nowhere near what I had been earning during the summer and my savings were not increasing as fast as I had hoped. I thought that I would never be able to afford my motorbike, let alone the insurance and everything else. I sent off for an exchange provisional driving licence to cover the motorcycle group, this cost me about two pounds, and seemed expensive considering I was only earning seven pounds and twenty-five pence a week now. Still, what does money matter if a dream becomes accessible. Only a couple more months and I would be old enough to own my first proper motorbike instead of just a moped. I could hardly wait, although I was beginning to wonder if I would still have enough money to buy one. However, it was up to me to keep saving to have any chance at all.

As my parents were having their own problems, the dreaded questioning never happened. They may not even have noticed that my friends would often happen to arrive on motorbikes instead of cars these days, as nothing was ever mentioned. I presumed they were too pre-occupied with themselves to worry about me, and I knew I was alright, so for the moment life kept running quietly as far as I was concerned. They knew that I didn't approve of smoking or drinking so maybe they assumed that I must be fairly sensible. Maybe they even thought I was boring as I would often say that I couldn't see what they saw in it all. My mum offered me a cigarette one night, and as most of my friends smoked I had a puff. It sent me most shades of green/purple/blue and nearly made me sick. Crazy habit. I wish she had just given me money, or better still, a motorbike instead.

Life goes on, and I had a nightlife to be getting on with. Our horizons had widened considerably during the year, and as well as still going to the dance halls, we would frequent several of the pubs and clubs in the nearby towns. On one such occasion we were sitting in a small disco/bar area and one of the fringe members of our acquaintance came over and joined in the general hub-bub of talk. He was generally well known, but as he was also known to indulge in various aforementioned iffy habits he was not actually a regular mate. It turned out that he needed some money and was trying to sell his old motorcycle. I asked some of the other lads what sort of bike it was. It turned out to be a 'James Captain'. It had a somewhat obscure sounding 198cc Villiers engine. Not knowing, or even having heard what that was, I was totally unimpressed, except for the fact that it had the right size engine and was already taxed and MOT tested, which made it legal to ride on the road. All I needed was the insurance. He was asking fifty pounds for it. This gave me food for thought, but as I couldn't picture the machine it didn't particularly bother or interest me unduly.

On reflection however, this episode did show me that I could lower my sights and look around for a second-hand machine. I spoke to some of the lads who were known to do their own bike maintenance and servicing and I asked if they would keep their ears open for me, as I would be interested if something suitable came up for grabs. Also, any advice they could give me as to what I could expect to pay for a machine. One lad mentioned the James, but said that although it was not being looked after properly it was a good sort of a bike. Being a two-stroke, it was quite a simple engine and maintenance should not be too hard or complicated. When told that the lad was asking fifty pounds for it, he said that was a bit steep anyway, and it was probably only worth about twenty-five or thirty pounds at the most, especially in its present condition. A bit more probing revealed that it would only take a week or so to get it cleaned up and looking smart. I asked if they would be prepared to help me with this if I bought the bike, as I was obviously unable to do anything like that myself just yet. On getting a positive response I decided to have a closer look at the bike when I next got the chance.

The grapevine did its work and the bike was duly down the café on the Sunday afternoon. I had a look at it but it looked quite plain and not at all like the gleamy bikes shown in the motorcycling magazines and papers that we all read at the time. However, the price was attainable. Being very undecided worked to my advantage as the price was quickly lowered to the thirty pounds. I was still unconvinced of the value though, and as he was so quick to come down it made me realise how desperate he was to sell. This raised doubts in my mind as I couldn't grasp why he was so eager to get rid of it, but on further investigation with some of the other lads, I was assured that the bike itself was a reliable machine. I left it as it was though, not committing myself either way. After all, it was the first big purchase of my own, and it was a bit daunting not being able to get some advice from my parents as I still had not dared mention my motorcycling ambitions to them. The problem also precipitated that point of no return when I knew it was time to face the parental position.

Thinking back to when we had lived abroad, it was the accepted thing to barter like hell when you wanted to buy anything. With this in mind, it gave me a distinct advantage knowing that the seller was keener than myself. If a deal was going to be made, it was going to be on my terms or not at all. Besides, it was quite a challenge to see how low the price might go. Maybe it would be alright after all, and with this in mind I decided to try for it.

Playing cool I didn't go out for a couple of evenings. My friends were all going out to a disco on Wednesday so I tagged along, having nothing better to do. The disco was a bit flat to start so we went across to the pub to see if any of the others were about. Dave was in there with one or two mates so we joined them for a while. After about half an hour the boy selling the James came in. He was quite wan, and asked if I had made up my mind regarding the bike. This opened up the haggling, him starting at the thirty pounds that he had already dropped down to. Within the opening round he quickly dropped down to twenty-five pounds. I tried for fifteen pounds which was half his starting figure. He dropped to twenty-two, I said that I only had eighteen pounds saved up. He cooled off and went out again. Maybe I was being a bit hard and I decided to go to twenty pounds when I next saw him. Within ten minutes though he came back and said that if I got the cash to him that evening, I could have it for eighteen pounds. Done. Hands shaken. The deal was agreed and Dave witnessed the fact. Dave also gave me a lift home to get the money as I did not have it with me. My parents weren't there so I escaped being questioned about being home so early. We got back to the pub, paid for the bike, and I was given the documents and keys for it. All that remained was to take it home and show mum and pops. We talked a friend into riding the bike home for me and installed it in the garage as quietly as possible. By this time the parents were home, and I hoped, in bed. The boys left and I went upstairs. As mum was in bed at least she wouldn't be too ready to go outside and look at it until morning; that would give her time to cool down, I hoped. Mum's light was still on so I went in to have a word with her. We talked for a little while before I dared bring up the subject. After several minutes of small talk and chatting, she said that as she was tired and would now like to get some sleep, would I mind telling her what I had wanted to talk about.

I almost froze as panic struck. I couldn't believe that she knew anything was on my mind. I asked what she meant? Her reply was that, as I never usually went in for cosy little chats there had to be something wrong and she said she would rather be told by me than by anyone else. I was somewhat surprised to think that she might know what I had done. I cast around in my mind trying to think who had told her anything, but I didn't think that she knew many of the lads I had been seeing in the last few weeks. I was somewhat het up to say the least, and I must have looked quite guilty as mum became quite agitated and said that I might as well tell her what was wrong, it was better out and in the open so that we could deal with things properly and in an adult manner. She was clearly trying to be calm and collected so I dropped my bombshell, but not the one she was thinking.

In trepidation, I started. "Mum, you'll never guess what I bought tonight" I blurted out? It was now mum's turn to be confused as she asked what it was I was trying to say? My reply that I had bought a motorbike was clearly not what she was expecting. "Oh," she said, "is that all?" She sounded quite relieved which now confused me. I then asked her what did she mean? Her reply that she thought I was going to tell her I was pregnant astounded me. After doing the majority of looking after my younger brother, now nearly 5 years old, that was the last thing I was going to do, saddling myself with responsibility before I had a chance to have a bit of fun, what was she thinking? After the initial relief wore off, she looked a little concerned about the motorbike, but I assured her it was only a little one, so that allayed fears a bit and she said she would have a look at it in the morning. Having expected to have a blazing row,

I went to bed, thankful that I had got off so lightly. Wonders will never cease.

The next morning I awoke with a start. Mum was yelling up the stairs for me to come down and explain the machine in the garage. She had gone out to look at what she had thought was only a little moped, and was rather taken aback to discover a vehicle which looked like a fully blown motorcycle. Did I really expect her to let me have a bike as big as that? And how was I going to learn to ride it without killing myself? She was not going to let me loose on that after my escapade with the car. Trying to give myself time to collect my thoughts (first thing in the morning has never been my best time of day), I put the kettle on and made a pot of tea, mum still rattling off all her endless objections. I did my best to remind her that we were going to discuss it in an adult manner, and was promptly balled out for daring to compare the situation. Don't adults have an annoying habit of only ever considering themselves as reasonable. After all, all I wanted was to be independent and self-sufficient, which I would have thought she should understand.

Once she had let off steam and realised that I was adamant about having my bike, we sat down and I told her most of the events leading up to the acquisition of the James. I obviously left out the colourful sections of my first few lessons, and I assured her that I would be very careful when I eventually went out on the road. She asked if I could take the bike back, but, as I pointed out, the lad had probably already spent the money, so that was out of the question. Resigned to the fact that the machine was to be a part of my life she asked me to introduce some of my latest friends to her. My stepfather then came in, surprising me more than ever by announcing that he thought it was a nice little machine, and started telling us both about some of the motorcycles that he had previously owned in his youth. After this sign of approval, mum capitulated, but she said that she would still like to talk about other things which would be cropping up in my life, now that I was obviously making decisions for myself.

Chapter 4

SHE IS A BAD INFLUENCE

Christmas was fast approaching and everyone seemed to be having parties. There was something happening most weekends and Wednesday nights were normally quite busy too. My friends thought I was weird because I would never drink alcohol and at one party they decided to bait me as being a wimp because I wouldn't touch the stuff. I got angry at not being left alone on this issue, so I challenged them all to try and drink me under the table if they thought they could. Having happily observed them for the last few months, I knew that none of them really drank much more than three or four drinks, and most used to then pretend to be pissed boasting of how many they had had, when in fact they had hardly had a drink at all. Having spent a lifetime watching my mother drinking very heavily, I had a good idea of what '*drinking*' looked like. My friends couldn't believe that Miss Teetotal would be able to drink them under the table, and as none could remember even seeing me touch a drink, the challenge was taken up on the condition that as it was so important for them to see me drink alcohol, it was up to them to pay for it.

The contest began, I surprised them by choosing Pernod with a touch of water, which they all thought was a strong drink. However, my ace in hand was that a couple of years beforehand, my family had been travelling across France and I had developed a liking for their local homemade aniseed drink, which was a lot stronger than Pernod. I drank mine steadily and after the first two measures when they had started being affected I discreetly poured most of my next five drinks into the pot plant behind my seat. No one noticed, and as they got the worse for wear, I was obviously still seemingly sober and able to walk in a straight line – and was promptly declared the winner. I did feel slightly guilty that I had more or less cheated my friends, but it solved the problem for me in that they then left me to drink my Coca Cola or Orange juices in peace and quiet. None of them ever called me a wimp again, and they were mostly astounded that a non-drinker was capable of seeing them off like that. I did confess to my closest friends soon afterwards, and we all had a bit of a giggle, but they understood my reasons for not wishing to drink alcohol in general. They could also accept me for who I was, and acknowledge the fact that I was mad enough sober, and probably best off without drink.

As the parties increased in frequency I came into contact with many new faces, and I soon learnt to recognise that the funny smoke smell was something called '*grass*'. Not to be confused with what one grew as a lawn. It just never seemed to do anything other than make people look and talk stupidly to my mind, and I could not get over seeing it as a waste of money for such a short-lasting thrill. From my point of view there was no reason to it, and it seemed a fruitless exercise. Some of the kids started spending all their money on this '*grass*' and it just seemed crazy to me to burn that money up with nothing to show for it. I couldn't see the point of normal cigarettes, but this craze appeared even sillier. Just because it was illegal didn't make it any more attractive in my eyes. I couldn't grasp the mentality of it all. I stopped going to some of the parties and went back to the dance halls, as I preferred to dance all night and really enjoy my life. Dancing was much more fun, and romance was easier if you knew that the object of your desire for the evening was really looking at you, and not some psychedelic Martian with green antennae, as one spaced out young man unfortunately described me one night. I liked to know exactly what I was doing, and didn't care for waking up with the worry of trying to remember if I had embarrassed myself, or upset anyone the previous evening, as some of my friends often did. Not knowing or remembering how they had got home was bad enough, but even worse was not getting home at all, finding themselves in extremely awkward situations the following mornings, and many an anxious month afterwards until their feminine bodies reassured them, or not. No, that was not the way I wanted my life to go.

The knowledge that I was in charge of my actions gave me a sense of power, and when it came to the boys in my life, they never stood a chance against my feelings of self-control and independence. All the macho-ness in the world is not worth the power a woman holds in her own actions and self-knowledge. I learnt early on that the woman is the one who is generally more selective and that it is an honour for a man to be the object of a girl's passion. Let's face it, very few men can refuse a girl once her desire is apparent, but the more obvious a man is about his desires, the less a girl is likely to be attracted to him. Funny that, but fun too, when used to one's own advantage.

I began to get pally with a girl called Barbara. She had only just recently moved to the area and didn't know anyone. She was drawn to our crowd as some of her previous friends had been motorcyclists, and she had more in common with us than with many of the seemingly namby pamby snooty girls who thought they were above such dirty habits as motorbikes and leather jackets. At first she appeared as just another face in the café, but as she started appearing regularly we soon started talking to her and letting her join in the various parties, escapades and adventures we got up to as a group. She was very funny and as I got to know her I found in her a kindred spirit. She wanted more out of life than just waiting for 'Mr Right' to come along on a white charger and whisk her off to wherever they are supposed to whisk a maiden off to. I never did work that one out, as it didn't look like there were many castles waiting for them; more like kitchen sinks. Anyway, Barbara was very surprised when I told her I had my own motorbike; a few days afterwards she came home with me to see it in daylight. We would sit and clean the bike together, looking forward to when I was old enough to actually get it on the road legally, and chatting animatedly of the time when we would be able to go up the road together in search of our own adventures and excitement.

I was naturally very flattered to be her heroine, even if it was only because I had actually gone out and bought my own bike. I just hoped she wouldn't be disappointed when it came to me riding on the road as I didn't think I would be able to ride as well as the boys (well, not to start with, but I had hope). I just accepted that to be totally independent would be enough for my own satisfaction, and meant everything to me. However, I was quite contented and blithely ignorant of the consequences of the extreme narrow mindedness of other people. Word soon got out that this girl was different. I soon became the target of much speculation and this worked both to my advantage, but also to my detriment. People may admire your spirit, but usually far more people will knock you either from their ignorance, or their jealousy, or their own inability to realise that it is not their position to judge anyone else for whatever reason. Much malicious gossip started and I was soon generally talked about, and considered by the old folks to be a bad influence on the town's young womenfolk, as I was 'fast' or even 'dangerous'; just because I had my own ideas and acted on them. One of the funnier sayings I heard levelled at me was 'being better than she should be'. In other words, I should know my position and stay there. I couldn't think why anyone would not want to achieve what they could, and what business it was of anyone else. If I worked and paid for what I wanted, as far as I was concerned it was my business. Even my friend

Barbara was told by her father that she was to stop seeing me because I was bound to lead her astray.

The thing that really bothered me most about all of this, was the total unfairness of it all. If only people would just let you live your own life, your own way. I couldn't believe how blind people were, only seeing what they wanted to see, and only hearing what they wanted to hear. I never expected anyone to do something just because I did. Indeed, I would have thought it weird if anyone had copied me, as I always had such strong convictions about my life and what I wanted from it, I just assumed that others did their own thing too. As for leading my contemporaries astray, it was just too ridiculous to even contemplate. Had anyone been prepared to look below the surface, then things may have looked very different from the view held by many of those parents. If most of the blinkered elders had taken the opportunity to talk to me and find out my reasons, perhaps more girls would have been encouraged to get their own vehicles, whether that was to be a moped, bike or car.

The reason why I bought the motorbike was not because I was bad, or wanted to shock, or to appear fast or cool. The reason was pure and simple in that I wanted my own transport, partly for the independence achieved, and partly so that I would not have to run the gauntlet of the increasingly persistent Romeos who had cars. It was getting harder and harder to get an acceptable lift home from the dances without incurring the usual advances which were getting harder to resist, as the boys in the group became more aware of what they desired as a trade-off; especially as they were now much stronger physically and knew what they wanted. Wandering hands were the norm with the more persistent lads but we soon learned ways of avoiding unwanted contacts. Personally, I found it much safer by far to have my own bike, and no amount of oldies pressure would persuade me otherwise. My father once described me aptly as 90% bullheaded mule.

The beneficial by-products of this independence were also largely ignored and totally misunderstood. As a girl's wages were always much less than guys generally commanded (often half their pay), it was harder for me to keep my bike on the road. Even if I had wanted to smoke, I could not afford cigarettes and petrol for my bike. Something I shall always be grateful for is that, by having my bike I was unable to start smoking and therefore I never had the problems later on experienced by my many friends as they were trying to give up this habit. The other major benefit was that I would not drink alcohol as this would not only affect my driving licence if I got stopped by the boys in blue, but I might run the risk of crashing my bike if I were ever drunk whilst out riding (balance being a major requisite). My independence was more important to me than anything else. Boy, am I glad now that it was? My only drug was the knowledge that I was free to come and go as I pleased, with no pressures to do anything that I wasn't ready for, and no having to trade favours for taxi fares.

Chapter 5

MAY I BE YOUR MECHANIC, PLEASE?

Being ever practical, it did not take me long to realise that on my wages I did not have much margin for emergencies such as mechanical breakdown, or indeed routine servicing and repairs. It did not seem right to expect the lads to do it for me, just because I was female. The only option was to learn to do things for myself.

It was obviously not within my financial power to have a spare bike to practice on, also, it was way beyond my abilities to buy a cheap box of parts in the profound hope that one day I would be inspired by these metal items into completing such a vast project. This train of thought led me to the conclusion that as much as I wanted to do such wondrous things with my life, I acknowledged a certain limitation in this course of action. Besides, if I could get into some sort of mechanical apprenticeship, I would solve two problems in one; I would be able to learn about my motorcycle and how to maintain it, and as there was no precedent I would probably be paid a normal male wage for a male job. Great. The problem now was to find a willing employer. The plan was good. Geography and timing were against me.

In my dream, I would walk into the required shop, chat to the boss, outline my plan and hey presto, motor mechanic extraordinaire is born. With my life's plan sorted I went out into the real world, full of optimism, and go-getting attitude.

I looked around the area for a suitable placement, and the only motorcycle shop within reasonable working distance was in a town about six miles away. It was close to the office where I was working, so during one of my lunchtimes I went around to the shop and had a word with the proprietor. He laughed at me, in a kindly but very patronizing way. Had it not occurred to me that women were meant to get married, have kids, and retire to become a housewife? In effect, his view of women was that they should gracefully become an appendage for a man, and basically our place was to retire from intelligent life, never to emerge again as an individual, but to know my place in society. Women, I was chided, were not made to be motorcycle mechanics. It did not make any difference to him that I had already proved I was different by actually having a motorbike of my own. I was told to not be so daft; anyone could see that it was only a fad, and that I would probably leave after the first year to have a baby, never to want another bike again. It would be a waste of everyone's time, and, more to the point, a bigger waste of his money.

I went away despondent, feeling very low but even more angry that he could scorn my ideas without even giving me a chance. Surely the fact that I had approached him with a sound scheme on my own should have been some sort of proof of the seriousness of my intentions and ambitions. His attitude was like a red rag to a bull (headed mule). I decided to lay siege to the shop and at every available free moment I returned to the premises to try and talk him round. I went in before work, during lunch breaks, and after work before heading home. I reasoned that eventually he would have a change of heart, and realizing how serious I was would give in and give me a job. However, after surviving this treatment for several weeks, I was the one who gave in: My siege wavered and I only went in about once a day, then every other day, and gradually tailed off. I was heartbroken and it knocked my confidence a bit to think that I was maybe not so appealing. I did not give up totally, although hope suffered enormously and waned. It annoyed me to think that the only reason he would not employ me was because I was female, and even worse, during one of my visits he actually conceded that if I had been a boy with my perseverance he would have snapped me up. That just beggared belief.

I still had the problem of how to overcome my initial need of doing my own motorcycle maintenance. My answer was 'get a book' to read up on it, and to this end I bought a book on simple mechanics and how the different engines worked, ie the difference between ordinary petrol engines, and then the vagaries of 2-stroke, diesel and even rotary principles. All very interesting. I then proceeded to read various books on the subject, all borrowed from the local library as I was not affluent enough to buy all that I wanted to read. Also, the iconic 'Haynes' had not yet invented his individual maintenance manuals yet. The first book I bought became my bible, as it was so simple to read; this was the Ladybird book in the 'How to…' series. It was only a cheap, very simplified book of engines and motorcycles, but it was thorough. It became my book of knowledge and I read it from cover to cover, re-read it from cover to cover, and re-re-read it from cover to cover.

This particular little book gave me knowledge. I discovered motorcycle maintenance and it became a long-time reference book for many years, as it described the various items and differences in a simple, straight forward understandable perspective, with really clear pictures and diagrams. I learned about magnetos, alternators, coils, plugs and points, chains and sprockets, all manner of interesting facets of these large lumps of metal. Joy of joys. Time and time again the little book proved invaluable in helping me to solve my motorcycle problems. The sheer simplicity of it was its best feature. It took me through the basic differences between two and four stroke engines, and how their strokes worked, to explaining all the various electrical gadgetry and gearing etc, in easy-to-understand terms and with particularly helpful diagrams. For all of its cheapness, it was superlative. However, as it was simply a general book and not a particular make book it gave a really comprehensive overall view of mechanics and maintenance. I was able to put this to good use and this cheered me up totally. I still hankered after an apprenticeship, but if it was not to be, I was quite happy about tackling all the simpler jobs on my own. I lost count of the times after than when I would dismantle things in a logical way, in order to re-assemble the awkward bits and bobs so that they would work again.

The greatest happiness, as I became more and more capable, was being able to keep up with the male conversations about bikes and cars and to understand their jargon when they tried to baffle me with the technical terms (BS). The more they tried to confuse me, the more I would go home and read up about the offending words until I became conversant enough to actually argue various points with them. The best was when I became competent enough to argue and actually win one or two battles of technicality.

A little knowledge was definitely a dangerous thing for me as I became quite vocal and a few of the lads got quite fed up with my particular brand of mechanism blended with feminine intuition and cussedness. This became my revenge on the world for not accepting a mere girl into the ranks of mechanicry. For all my newfound abilities and noisiness, I really enjoyed pulling some of the lads up when they obviously didn't know what they were talking about. Gradually as they realised that when I joined in their chatter and banter I was not quite as dumb as they liked to think I was. I became more accepted and as well as feeling happier with myself, the boys started to welcome my input as I always thought outside of the box – and often my hunches proved good – and more importantly, they usually worked. Funny that, the more you learn about something, the less you have to prove. I found that as time wore on I was laughed at less and less, and actually encouraged more and more, to the point where my contributions on possible problems were actually sought and acted upon. This is where feminine intuition helped most of all.

I lost count of the number of times where I made my most brilliant contributions to projects using no more than calculated guesswork to solve problems which were defying my peers. As is often the case, some of my most inspired guesses worked best, confounding some of the more experienced mechanics amongst us, (but remember, we were all learning and finding our way) but it confirmed my place within the group. Of course, when farfetched but useable contributions were made, I never would admit how I had known it would work, a mysterious smile and evasion pushed my street cred through the roof.

My new-found knowledge became the basis of a game we started playing while sitting in the local pub in the neighbouring town, with a great group of mates. The pub was in a narrow back street and we started by listening to the bikes passing outside. We began by guessing whether the bike which had just been ridden up the street was a two-stroke or four-stroke, which was relatively easy as the two-strokes usually had an empty can sound, with varying degree of insect noise inside it; making it either screechy or just pure tinny. The four-strokes were generally a lot deeper sounding, and much kinder to the ears. The next progression of this game was to try to work out if the bikes were one, two, three or four cylinders. This also made variations of sound, a one cylinder machine would have a slower 'thump' or 'whine' to it, and more cylinders would produce quicker notes – leading to different makes also having different sounds. British bikes also being an even deeper thump or growl as their casings were of a heavier casting. Over the course of the summer, we became adept at not only recognising type of engine, but also makes of bike, one of us standing at the door to corroborate whether we had guessed correctly. Eventually we were able to discern not only make and model of bike, but also whose bike it was by the way the bike was ridden, eg the way they used throttle, gears, braking etc. I have always had a good ear for language, voice recognition and tone, so I became very good at this – much to my surprise and enjoyment. Finding fun was always a plus in my book.

During this period I was still going into the motorcycle shop, but the owner was still adamant that girls could not be mechanics, no matter how much I badgered him. Nevertheless, towards the end of the year on one of my visits to his shop I noticed a poster on the wall advertising a coach trip to London, to the Racing and Sporting Motorcycle show. This intrigued me and I asked about this trip and signed up for a place on the bus. I paid for my ticket over a couple of weeks as it was not cheap, but it looked exciting; I had to go. The time soon passed by and I duly got up at five o'clock to get to the bus on time. This was worth the effort, as yet again I met a lot of different people, mostly guys again, and the whole day was a great change and I was spell-bound. There was about 45 people who went, all of them in a great mood, and hellbent on having a good time for the day. Most of them were astounded that a slip of a girl would go on her own, and they became quite protective of me. When they found out I had my own bike they were surprised, but also very encouraging and supportive. Being mostly a bit older than my mates, it was fun as they exchanged their stories of escapades, scrapes and ride outs together.

On the way we stopped at a transport café on the A11 for breakfast and toilet break, the Red Lodge Café. In the early 1970s this was very basic, and the loos were set up in ramshackle sheds behind the café – not very clean but at least it had walls and some sort of roof. The clientele was mainly truck drivers and bikers as it was not really a family stopover. But they did serve good bacon and egg breakfasts, and a good cup of tea. This café became a regular haunt of mine with or without my mates ever after. We had a thirty minute stop before it was back on board for the show.

Despite a long queue to get into the halls at Lambeth, I spent the day absolutely enthralled at the amount of extras that could be bought, all the different types of motorcycle shops, engineers showing their skills which could be bought; clothing; bike stands for all the different makes showing this year's models and those being displayed ready for the following year. One of the chaps on the bus, Roger, bought himself one of the new 'full-face' crash helmets and proudly showed it off on the return bus trip. Many of the group showing off their purchases on the trip home, excitedly talking about the various modifications they were making to their machines, clip ons; shiny footrests; sissy bars; higher bars; Norton straight bars; higher specification brake pads; you name it, they had bought it. One of the men had even bought himself a full fairing for the front of his bike. It looked like a sail to me, but hey ho, we all have our foibles, luckily the bus driver had put this into the luggage hold underneath the passenger floor, so it could be taken home. The whole day was an experience of the wider world, not to be forgotten. The return trip was quieter as we were all extremely tired after all the excitement and walking about, and we did a return stop for food at the Red Lodge, where half went into the café and the other half into the pub next door. We all had our meals and drinks, and eventually got home about 11:30 that night. And I had a whole new group of friends.

Chapter 6

ONE OF THE LADS

It always amazed me how good it felt when I was actually able to help the lads with their problems. I enjoyed the camaraderie of joining in with the lads on their terms and as we developed our various pecking orders, I managed to help out more and more with various projects, learning more and more all the time. It was always fun to join in and the muckier I got, the happier I was. Also, by being there to help them, gave me access to their workshops and equipment which I had no hope of having for myself, so it was a definite win/win situation all round. As an extra pair of hands were always welcome when working on their projects I got an ever-increasing circle of male friends. This in itself caused me much amusement as many of the more conventional girls in the area couldn't understand how I could be so popular covered in dirty black oil, when their own well-manicured and well-groomed selves were passed by. Many of the local girls could not accept that a girl could be just 'one of the lads' and I found it quite hilarious that they could think I was after their blokes. The reason I was doing it all was so that I didn't need a bloke, when I had so many mates.

The general mentality of folk at the time seemed very blinkered to me, and I fueled the gossip quite happily; I reasoned that if they were talking about me they were probably leaving some other poor soul alone, so I really wasn't too bothered about the many jibes and remarks which would come my way. I soon learnt how to deal with the various petty jealousies and inuendo's with a daft remark, usually guaranteed to annoy further, or to turn the stupidity back on the giver. This again fueled my own sense of confidence, realising that to be happy, I just had to be happy, and rise above those who tried to put me down. My own view of myself was all that mattered to me.

Going around in a group meant that there was always something going on and there were enough escapades and happenings amongst us to keep us all amused. One particular episode in this period stands out. It was when Kevin decided to put his sidecar back on his bike. This caught my attention, as it was a new job to get our heads around, and more knowledge to learn. Several of us arranged to get together down the shed and Andy, another of our mates, found and brought an old manual with instructions on how to fit a sidecar properly.

Apparently it was not a case of:-

1) get bike
2) get sidecar
3) bolt sidecar to bike
4) ride off into sunset.

It was much more technical than that.

The bike apparently has to be angled outwards a certain degree – just slightly – so that when the sidecar is occupied the bike is then pulled back inwards and will handle better under load, (which is why a sidecar is often weighted when nobody is riding shotgun). This is the idea and there was a lot of squit talked about, and done, but with the help of Kevin's father's spirit level and plumb line, and various other tools from his shed, we finally thought the job complete. All that remained was to road test the final product.

In view of my previous mishap with the sidecar, I was relegated to the chair, Andy rode pillion and Kevin was pilot as it was his bike after all. The sidecar was extremely basic, being a box type of affair, with only a cushion for a seat, however there was a grab rail around the front of the chair. I decided that so that I could see better I would kneel, holding onto the grab rail. This is where someone ought to have told me that when in the chair it is better to not see where one is going, and better still, to sit still as dead weight. I just didn't realise how crucial it is to lean properly without upsetting the balance whilst cornering. With this minor detail unwisely left unsaid, naively, expecting to have a straightforward run, and indeed, at first it was fun. However, once Kevin got used to the sidecar again, he got a bit more adventurous and started travelling a little quicker. This was fine, I always enjoyed a bit of speed, but as we got faster, bearing in mind my last effort near the bridge, I began to get a touch nervous. I told Kevin to slow down a bit as we were now on a smaller road. Kevin, enjoying the fact he had the upper hand, and laughing at my rare discomfiture, to prove his competence and boost his own ego, rode quicker still. This would in itself have been alright, but as we approached a rather tight left-handed bend, I took fright. Thinking we were going to go up the inside bank, I jumped onto the back of the bike. In the ensuing panic, there was a mad scramble; people changing places. Kevin yelled at me as he leapt into the chair in a frantic attempt to re-balance the outfit, leaving Andy suddenly as pilot. The culmination was an extremely crumpled heap of metal and bodies as we launched forth through the hedge, over the ditch the other side, and into yet another ploughed field.

After the initial shock died down, we dragged the outfit back out and onto the road. Luckily, other than knocking the forks out of line, there did not seem to be any real damage to anything other than my popularity. Again, a few rather heated exchanges ensured about who was the biggest idiot, we managed to limp home with the machine, but I was forever banned from all further contact with Kevin's beloved sidecar outfit. I was quite happy about that anyway; I had rather gone off them by this time as I obviously didn't get on with them. Two crashes out of two rides was not a good record. As you can imagine there was a lot of mileage to be had out of that crash, and the boys reveled in my demise. Various lads recommended I try tractor driving in future, considering my homing instinct for ploughed fields. Still, as I was far from being the only person to crash (although it seemed so to me for a while), I was not cast out of the group and it gave us more to talk and laugh about. I learned the importance of not taking events too seriously, and most importantly, have the ability to laugh at myself. That lesson has been invaluable, as no-one is perfect, and when things go wrong, it imprints on your memories and are a good source of entertainment later on.

One of my mates around this time was renowned for riding too close to the rider in front, and this provided us with further entertainment. Whilst out for a ride one afternoon, a couple of the lads had lagged behind and were trying to catch us up. On this particular stretch of road there were several really great bends, some of them really tight but brilliant for honing our 'racing' lines etc. Denny was as usual riding close up behind Michael, who was optimistic about his Hailwood skills (Mike 'the bike' Hailwood being the best motorcycle racer of all time, in my opinion). Michael took one very awkward bend far too fast, totally misjudged the bend and had the choice to either crash into the farm wall, or not. His decision was an out-of-control chaotic skid and slide into the farmer's yard and barn through the open doors, coming to an almost graceful halt. Not to be outdone, Denny gaily followed Michael's disastrous route into the barn, just managing to avoid hitting Michael and neatly parked up beside him. This caused endless hilarity, with various comments like 'funny choice of companion for rolling in the hay' or 'first time I heard of anyone egg-collecting on motorcycles'. It all helped take the brunt of the jokes and sarcasm away from me.

Chapter 7

IDLE TALK DOES HURT

As my seventeenth birthday came and went, another major phase in my life happened. It partly arose because of the adult suspicions that I was 'not a nice girl' because I was one of them 'greasers' as the term was at the time for most motorcycle lads. The view gently pervaded through the village, and some of the supposedly respectable lads in the area. My biking friends knew better, but they too were 'a bad influence' just because of the bikes, and I guess the many escapades we were responsible for.

One of the first things that jolted me from my naïve existence was when I came into contact with a local man called Pete, who was about 24 or 25 years old. He was well-known in the area and I had been warned to steer clear of him as he was known to be real trouble, with a bad attitude to everyone. He had apparently been in prison before, notably for beating up on an ex-girlfriend. I would always treat people as I found them, so although wary of him, I spoke if he did, but I never actually sought his company and deliberately avoided him where possible. He mixed with a different crowd so that was not too hard to do. However, one afternoon as I was going to the local café, he saw me and fell into step with me. He asked me to go for a walk with him to the local park. When

I declined he got really angry, took my refusal as a personal affront, accusing me of being a tart and a slag among other equally horrible things. The culmination of it all was that he threatened to rape me, all he had to do was to grab hold of me one night and I wouldn't stand a chance. I didn't doubt him. This did frighten me somewhat as I knew he meant it, and I certainly did not want my first experience of blanket hurdling to be a violent one. I took his threat seriously and knew I had to do something. I couldn't understand why he had singled me out this way, especially when I had never even encouraged him in any way.

After thinking the problem through I came to the conclusion that the best plan of action would be to choose someone for myself, and take the fear of the unknown away. At least then I could take control and this event would be on my own terms, and if the worst came to the worst I would have some idea of what to expect. With more than a little trepidation, I set about looking for a likely subject. This was harder than you could imagine for although there were many possibilities, I still wanted the event to be a bit special, and more than just a one-night stand.

The first boy who caught my interest was Billy, but after kissing and cuddling during the evening, when we started getting a bit more serious, he was like a bull in a china shop. That was it. I made an excuse to stop and then fled. I didn't think it would be so difficult. Surely it wasn't too much to expect some consideration at a time like that. I was a lot more careful choosing the next potential object of my onerous intention. I also had learned a valuable lesson in that it is not as easy for an inexperienced lad to slow down once he was excited, and nor do they listen at that point. An old saying mentions 'when blood is up' and I now knew what they meant. I was a lot more careful about choosing the next object for my intended experience.

I went back to my biker friends and started eyeing up the available talent there. There were two or three that I quite liked amongst them, so I set to work vetting their various charms, attractions, credentials and availability. I did not want to intrude on anyone else's relationships. One of the lads, Ben, seemed suitable so I singled him out for my attention. He seemed amiable enough, and having been very friendly with one of his previous girlfriends I knew he had some experience in the necessary department. Thinking this over, I deducted that at least he would know what he was doing. With the proposed target in view, I now had to plan the where, when, and how. This is where providence came to my aid in the shape of my parents going down to London for an all-night party. Great. But was it all going too smoothly, I wondered? Putting my concerns aside, I realised I now had the where, and when. My campaign was getting under way, and I now had a fortnight for the planning.

I started the flirtation up straight away, no sense in wasting time. The other thing on my mind was the pregnancy thing. Remembering the quotation 'prevention is better than cure' I made an appointment to see my doctor to counter this problem. It was just my luck that my doctor was a Catholic. He was definitely old school, and not impressed with my desire to go on the pill. Even worse, he was most upset when he found out that I did not already have a boyfriend but was prospecting. When he realised I was actually actively intent on losing my virginity as I had not actually started on any sexual activities, well, he hit the roof. He gave me such a lecture on how silly I was to even think of contraception, and just gave me a scathing look when I said that I wanted to start that side of my life. As I was seventeen, at least he wouldn't be able to go behind my back and tell my parents.

This did set me back, so plan B had to found. The only alternative was to get some condoms from the chemist. This proved to be a fairly humorous occurrence. I decided that as the parents knew the local pharmacists I would have to go to somewhere anonymous myself, and hence took a train to the City about twenty miles away to find a chemist shop. In those days it was not the done thing to display condoms openly and you had to ask the counter assistants to get them for you. I was a bit unsure of myself and waited for the shop to be as good as empty before approaching the staff and with a bit of bluff and bluster asked for a packet of 'rubbers'. The lady was helpful, but when she asked me what size did I need, it nearly threw me. I mean, how was I to know? I must have looked a bit confused, and she suggested that perhaps I should go for the middle size. I agreed, and made my purchase. I turned and was about to leave when I noticed a young man approach the same lady and ask for a box of 'French letters'. As I knew that was another name for condoms I couldn't help but observe his obvious shyness, and the look of the woman was quite mischievous. She got out a full box (of about 20 rubbers) and innocently asked if that would be enough. The chap coloured up and said yes, how much? As he paid, the other assistant popped over and said, that must be some party you're going to! The man grabbed his purchases and left in a hurry, whereupon we all three had a good giggle. I think this was a slightly rehearsed gag between the two of them, and was thankful they had not subjected me to that joke.

With everything else set up and ready, the only thing left was to manoeuvre Ben into the right frame of mind. No problem. We got through the kissing stage easily enough, and I realised he was fairly keen as he kept coming back for more. The idea now was to keep him simmering until the appropriate night. To make sure Ben was available on the night in question, I said I had been invited to a party and would he go with me. Like a lamb to the slaughter...

The next part of the plan was to get some books from the library about these things and, although I did not really know what would happen, I still needed to feel in control. Having read a few appropriate books avidly I found out it was best if I was relaxed and comfortable for the occasion. After all, the whole point of this was so that I did not have a bad experience for my first event. Also, I did not want to appear ignorant, especially as I was going to be in charge of matters. I was beginning to actually enjoy instigating my romance, as I knew exactly where it was going to end, I was in total control. I thought. Poor Ben, little did he suspect of my extremely devious intentions, I kept thinking how funny it would be when he realised that I was not just leading him on, but fully committed. In the meantime I was learning quite a bit about my own feelings and responses, not least because I was actually very attracted to him in that way. Fascinating subject, I sifted through my books, discarding many ideas as stupid fantasy, but storing up any snippets which might be of use to me. The whole idea was taking off quite well, I could hardly wait for the great occasion.

The Saturday finally arrived and it seemed to take ages for the parents to go – at one point when they got arguing about the route and where to go – I thought everything would fall flat and there weren't going to go at all. My sister and I duly waved them off, wishing them a good time and not to worry as we would be alright. Mother looked a bit concerned but didn't say anything. I felt as though I were a race horse, waiting at the starting gate and all of a sudden up went the gate and off I went. The remainder of the day became a bit like a rollercoaster, once started, it was difficult to stop the excitement and turbulence within, and even more difficult to get off. Even so, with all the events and planning leading up to this night, I was more than ready, but as a safeguard I did not mention to anyone that my parents were away. My sister knew what I was up to and she kept her head down and out of the way. She couldn't believe I would actually go ahead, but was also dying to know the outcome, good job I could trust her. Tonight was the night and we were meant to be alone, nothing was going to upset it. Or so I thought.

Ben arrived looking really quite presentable, all spruced up and with a tough of Brut on. At least he had unwittingly made an effort. As I had a very slim figure at that time, I had on a very tight-fitting mini skirt and skinny rib jumper, which although were not the latest fashion suited my purpose for the evening. With my knee-high black platform boots on I thought I looked just the ticket. I told Ben the party had been cancelled but that we could still go to the dance or pub if he was happy to. We went to the dance as he felt a bit too dressed up for the pub. We had a good time, I made him dance a couple of smoochies near the end of the night, holding him closer than I had previously dared. We then went home, Ben coming in for a 'coffee'. By this time I was more than sure of him and there was no way I would have turned back on my plan now. As for Ben, well, hook, line and sinker.

When we got back home I put the kettle on, but the coffee never got made. We were in the living room having a fairly heated hug and kissing session, and when I thought that he was fit to burst, I made an excuse to go upstairs to the bathroom. Once upstairs I called him up, supposedly to catch a spider, he duly came upstairs as quietly as he could thinking my parents were perhaps in bed already, or if not, likely to be home any time now as it was already past midnight. When he saw that I was in their room, sitting on the double bed, he looked petrified. I said it was alright and told him they were not coming home that night, and to close the door behind him. His face was a picture. Totally bemused, not sure that he had heard right, but also sure he had. He was rather taken aback but recovered quickly and took full advantage of the situation. His final shock, when it dawned on him that I had planned the whole seduction, was when I produced the condoms. By that time it was too late for him to change his mind and I had my way with him.

After all that, the actual event was not at all how I had imagined it, and if any impression was made at all, it was just that the whole thing was a bit of an anti-climax (no pun intended) but thankfully not unpleasant. There was no sudden orchestral music in my ears, no earthshattering happenings. I honestly couldn't make out what all the fuss was about. It really is just another thing that happens in life.

The biggest excitement of the night was when my parents returned home about five o'clock in the morning. Ben and I woke up with a start when the car doors slammed shut. Mum was already in the house and on her way up the stairs. There was no escape as their bedroom door was immediately at the top of the stairs, we were trapped. There was no escape and as mother opened her bedroom door, Ben hid under the duvet pulling it up over his head. She put the light on and looked me straight in the eyes.

"Err… Hello Mum, …er, this is Ben," I said!

She called down to my stepfather to put the kettle on, she would be down in a minute. She then ordered Ben into my bedroom and told me to help her change the sheets on her bed. Once Ben had gone into the other room, mum asked me what I thought I was playing at. I told her it was alright, we hadn't done anything stupid, meaning that we had used precautions. It was then my turn to be embarrassed as her response was that "you have just missed a bloody good chance then!". Later that morning we had a really good talk, she was surprisingly calm about things, and even had a laugh at my bad luck at the doctor's. However, she promptly took me back to the surgery where we saw a different doctor who put me on the pill. My mother's response was not the usual for parents of that time, but that is another story altogether.

The next time I saw my antagonist, Pete, I was really angry with him because of his stupid threats, but with my newfound confidence about such matters I tackled him head on. I found him in a café which I knew was his usual haunt for himself and his sidekicks. I told him quite loudly and angrily exactly what I thought of him and his threats, and that I had now tried sex and how I felt it was over-rated and that there was nothing in it to write home about. By my manner and what I said, he realised that I was not what he had thought, and he told me why he had taken my refusal as a personal snub. The local talk was that I had already slept with most of the local lads, and as I was supposedly so easy, he was angry that I didn't want to know him. He apologised to me when I told him what had happened because of his threats to me, and I left with him having more respect for me after that.

When I finally got to the bottom of the original rumours, it turned out that it had been started by a lad whom I had known for about eighteen months and had thought was a good friend. The whole thing had been the result of this one young man's idle boast. Mike was great fun to be with and as I had known him for quite a while I felt very comfortable and easy in his company. We would get talking on just about any subject you could imagine and I considered him a friend. One day, after lying on the beach most of the morning, we climbed the cliffs. It started as a dare, and I surprised him by actually reaching the top before him. We sat down to catch our breath before setting off again. The sun was shining and we went for a walk along the cliff top, gaily chatting away as we went. There was no hint of romance, not even a kiss, we were just mates.

However, when quizzed by a couple of his mates after that, he pretended that of course, 'we had gone all the way'. This stupid lie had a snowball effect, and some of the other lads who were later seen in my company added to it, just to 'puff up their own egos'. It could have easily turned out disastrously different if I had been a more timid girl. I was so angry I became determined to have my revenge, and clear my name at the same time.

When Mike heard that I was gunning for him he stayed out of my way for a couple of months, but thinking that my anger had died down, he ventured back to one of the local clubs. Sure enough, a mutual acquaintance tipped me off that he was at the disco. With a trail of mates in my wake, some trying to calm me down and talk me out of doing anything daft, some not wanting to miss anything, I descended on the club, pushing the bouncers out of my way, I stormed through to the disco floor, my temper got the better of me and I exploded. The language was not repeatable, but the meaning very clear. I confronted Mike with his lie, and stated loudly that the next bloke to lie about his conquests should beware the victim. With that last remark over loud and clear, I swung my fist and floored Mike unexpectedly with the first blow. With that, as he lay on the floor under the disco lights, I glared at everyone else, daring anyone to even think about helping him up, and told him that another time he had better think before starting such stories and I left the room. Apparently, he went bright red, pathetically held his jaw and left, looking very sheepish and extremely sorry for himself. He did not dare come near me again for a long while. Just as well because it had been no joke for me either. Having not seen me in a temper before, my friends realised that although generally I was very happy go lucky, if anyone rocked my boat, come hell or high water I would sink theirs. My self-respect was back intact, my reputation cleared.

Chapter 8

DOWN TO EARTH WITH A BUMP

Having a bike on the road legally was really great, and I did many miles on my little machine. It was fantastic to be able to go out of the house, hop on my bike and not have any restrictions on where I could go. Friends and relatives had to put up with me arriving at any time of night or day. I reveled in not having to keep clockwatching in case of missing the last bus home, and not having to worry about walking the odd few miles between villages where buses never went. The total freedom was great, and when I found a road I didn't know, I would try it out, just to do a few more miles and see another place. I wanted to go everywhere that I had been unable to go only days earlier. I wanted to see every little nook and cranny in the surrounding countryside, just because I had never before been able to. The only thing I could think of that could beat this feeling would be to flap ones arms and fly, but that was obviously an impossible dream.

I rode the James about for approximately two months and enjoyed every moment. I had one or two minor mishaps, bending the odd footpeg or four, but mostly managed to keep on the road and in one piece. The only problem was that as it was an old bike it would occasionally turn temperamental on me. It was also not always easy for me to kickstart, especially first thing in the morning.

I was not spending so much on bus fares everywhere so I was able to still put a little money to the side. I also got a wage rise at work which helped enormously. With the newfound wealth it seemed logical to try and update my machine with a more modern version. A friend of mine was selling his Honda CB175 which was only 3 years old. It seemed a good motorcycle and was very shiny and attractive, it had a 175cc twin cylinder engine and an electric start. I already had nearly fifty pounds in my savings again and I started thinking. The Honda was going for about a hundred pounds. My James, now that it had been cleaned up, looked tidy and was maybe worth thirty pounds. On checking the insurance, there was no difference in price as I was insured for up to 200cc and the cover would automatically transfer as I had what was called a 'rider policy'. Tax and MOT costs would be the same too. It looked like it would be a good buy if I could raise the remaining monies.

The parents were resigned to me riding a motorcycle by now, so I approached my stepfather and mother, explaining the situation and showing how it made sense to have a newer machine. They were hesitant at first, but then they agreed to lend me the remaining money, as long as I paid them back at one pound every week, this would take twenty weeks, just under five months. This seemed a good deal, but my stepfather wanted to inspect the bike to be sure it was suitable. I agreed to this and I arranged for the bike to be brought home to my house and put the word out that my James was for sale at thirty pounds. (I had learned the great art of bargaining when we had lived abroad for a couple of years.)

The Honda was brought round to the house a couple of days later, and after a thorough inspection a provisional agreement was made to buy the bike, so long as the lad would wait for me to sell my James. My friend was selling the Honda to buy a larger bike as he had recently passed his test. He walked back to me and suggested that he could take the James as a part exchange for twenty-five pounds if I was interested. Thinking about the savings on advertising and possibly missing the chance of the Honda if it didn't sell quickly, I asked my stepfather if he could up his loan to me for the extra five pounds, and he agreed to do so. Obviously my payments would be extended, but the exchange was agreed and we swapped bikes, monies and documents. Yippee, I was now the proud owner of a pretty golden yellow Honda.

My older sister was still living abroad at that time, but had come home for a holiday. She was amazed to see her young sister so much more mature, she took a couple of pictures of me on my Honda, she laughed at the fact that I was now old enough to have a motorcycle and happily gave me tips for riding, as she had a moped to get around where she lived. In her mind I was still a 'kid' sister at school, so to see me so grown up was funny for her to get her head round. It was the first time we had been able to talk on an equal footing and it was lovely to have that time with her, as we had been apart for about five years by then. Mind you, I had always been a 'tom boy' so she was not that surprised at my wanting a boy's toy.

I was over the moon about my new machine, and my conversation at work was all about my bike, my friend Karen was particularly keen to see my new steed. I phoned her up and told her that I would be riding it to work on Monday so that she could see it. She never managed to see it in one piece though. On the Monday morning I got all dressed up and set off out. I got the bike out of the garage, packed all my gear onto it, got on and pressed the electric start. Whrrrrrr Whrrrr Whrr Wr Wr Wr oh S***. The electric start would not start it. I couldn't think what had happened. It had been starting up all right, no problems all weekend. I checked it all over and realised I had left the lights on all night. I tried the kick start but after several attempts it still would not work, so I decided to try and bump start the thing. Just down the road from us was a sloping hill. I pushed the bike to the hill and got on. Putting it into second gear and holding the clutch in, I scooted it to start the momentum downhill. I dropped the clutch and WHAM, at last it fired into life, but in my fright about keeping the engine running I opened the throttle too much and shot forward, overshooting the junction out into the next road. It was a blind corner and as I came out of my side road, a car came from my right-hand side and hit me side on.

At first, as I flew over the top of the car, I looked down at the roof of the vehicle. It seemed to take ages before I fell to the ground and all I could think of was that 'I can fly' I imagined that I was dreaming, but I soon came down with a nasty bump. Lying on the road beside the car, the driver then got out and started shouting at me. I retaliated, only being worried about the state of my bike, I was now a mangled heap in the road.

I picked myself up, turned off the engine which was surprisingly still running, but I couldn't move it to the side of the road. Some passersby helped to move it out of the way and put it up on the pavement, against a garden wall. I then promptly fell over and when I couldn't get up again, realised I had hurt my leg. The car driver then started shouting at me again, and we had a row, someone else by then had recognised me and phoned my mum. I looked at my bike and burst into tears, I had wrecked my beautiful new machine.

Mum promptly arrived and was relieved to hear me shouting. Finding that I had only hurt my leg she set about exchanging addresses etc and took me to hospital in her car. My older sister came too, lecturing me in her big sister manner. I felt so stupid. I was maybe not so clever at all. I was by this time too upset and probably in shock, I was unable to argue back. All I could think about was my poor bike, lying there, at the side of the road on its own. Why, oh why, did this have to happen? Why, oh why, did I leave the lights on last night? Did I really deserve this sort of luck?

On arrival at the hospital I was sent for the usual X-rays, and spent the next couple of hours feeling as sick as a pig, my pride hurting from my sister's nagging. I know this was out of worry for me, but it didn't help me feel any better having all my faults flagged up in public. Mum just took it all in her stride and didn't say too much. It was all too much for me though, and I couldn't stop the tears. The hospital said that I had been lucky but had torn the ligaments in my right knee. They wanted to do a small operation to sew them up again and I would have to stay in overnight. Mum signed the necessary papers and after seeing me into the ward where I would be going, she and my sister went home. I was taken down to the operating theatre soon after their departure, and after having an injection I passed out.

When I woke up it was late afternoon, and was starting to get dark. I looked to see what they had done and found my right leg in a full-length plaster cast. I then looked around the ward to see what it was like. It was very dismal. There were only four beds in the room, but the other occupants were a lot older than me. The bed at the foot of mine was occupied by a lady who I couldn't see very well, but I could hear her only too well, I could hear her making sighs and moans – obviously in a lot of pain. The lady to my right was in plaster casts and bandaging from head to toe, she was also strung up so much that she barely had more than three square inches touching the bed. It was as if she was only allowed that much touch in order to stop her swinging to and fro. I thought they ought to have given her a hammock. The fourth bed was empty.

Teatime came and went; my mum and sister came up to visit me. They brought in a couple of books and some fruit, but all I wanted was some clothes to go home in. This was not allowed as having just had a general anesthetic I was to be kept under observations for at least twenty-four hours. This was the first time I had ever been in hospital and I was not impressed at all. Especially as the lady at the foot of my bed was mysteriously removed during the night. I had my suspicions but no-one would confirm what had happened to her. If that wasn't bad enough, after taking all night to get to sleep, I could only have slept about an hour when the tea ladies breezed in brightly asking if we wanted a cup of tea. Asking the time, I was told it was a quarter to six in the morning. My request to be left alone to sleep was ignored, and I was sat up with my cuppa, like it or not, my pillows plumped and there was no hope of getting any sleep after that. When the doctor came round I asked when I would be allowed home, and she answered if all was well I could be collected mid-afternoon. I asked for the telephone machine to be brought round the ward to me, and I phoned and asked mum if she could collect me, as I didn't want to be there any longer than I had to. As soon as she arrived I grabbed my clothes and the crutches I had been given, mum duly signed me out and we left.

Chapter 9

ON THE ROAD AGAIN

Being a naturally happy person, I did not stay in the dumps for long, and who could be, when I had so many friends who would come round with all sorts of goodies. Most of them would stay for a while and it was nice to hold court at home and have others running around for me. I made the most of the next few weeks as best I could, and it was extremely comforting to know that I had friends who wanted to come and spend time with me. It was irksome that I could not go out to any of the dances while I had my leg in plaster, but there was no lack of gossip as most of my friends would be bursting to tell me all about what was going on.

I had been told to go back to the hospital after five weeks to have my plaster cast removed, but as mum was not willing to take me, the hospital arranged for me to have a hospital car to get me there (this was a volunteer run scheme for people in our rural area who either did not have buses or other transport readily available). I was very grateful to be collected from home, but he had not been told I had a full-length plaster cast on, so it was a bit difficult to get me into the car. I could not sit with the leg across the back seat as there would be another person to sit there. I had to sit on the back left hand rear seat with my leg down between the two front seats, propped up on some cushions to keep it clear of the handbrake and gear levers. It was very uncomfortable, but, as it was the only transport available for me, I had to put up with it, for 28 miles.

Never mind, after driving a lengthy route through several villages to pick up the other two patients, we got on our way. The whole palaver took about one and a half hours by the time we got to the hospital. As I was a bit late for my appointment in casualty, it was a further two hours and I still had not been seen by the doctor. The other two people in the hospital car had by this time both been to their departments and were ready to go home. The driver was agitated and asked if I would be able to get alternative transport home? I said yes and let him go as I still did not know how long I was going to be kept waiting, and it wasn't really fair to expect others to wait for me unnecessarily.

As it turned out, I was kept waiting for a further two hours before I was seen, and instead of having my plaster off as I expected, I was told I would have to have another one on for a further three weeks. This was a bit of a blow as I thought I would be walking out normally. I tried ringing mum, but she was still not home, and it was too late to arrange another hospital car to get me home and I would have to go home by bus. This was easier said than done, not expecting this I did not have any money for a bus or train nor did I have anyone to borrow from. I was stuck, nearly thirty miles from home, with a leg still in plaster, hobbling along on crutches. There was only one thing for it, and despite BT recommending all and sundry to walk on their fingers, I had to resort to my trusty thumb, and hitch hike home.

In order to get on the right road, I first had to walk about a mile and a half through the City, and once there I put my trusty digit to work. It must have been a strange sight to behold, me standing on the side of the road, on crutches, with a leg in full length plaster. The first few cars passed by, probably thinking it was a sketch from 'Candid Camera' a television show popular at the time, and obviously did not want to stop. The first few cars went by probably thinking that I was some sort of weirdo, others may not have stopped – not believing their eyes – or otherwise maybe realising the trouble it would take to get me in the car as I was obviously not going to be easy to load up. I thought I was never going to get home, I was tired, and all I wanted now was to get home and lay down.

I must have been there a good twenty minutes before a truck driver stopped and offered me a lift. The first problem was how to get up into the lorry. However, luckily I did not weigh very much (about seven stone) but the chap was strong enough to be able to pick me up and put me into the cab. The relief at being able to sit was great, and there was enough room for me to put my leg across the seat as there were three seats across the front. This was great, not only did I have a lift which was reasonably comfortable, but he took me all the way home in the truck. I soon cheered up again, and far from feeling fed up with my day, it turned around and gave me a completely new experience seeing the road from so high up. Life is curious the way it swings up and down, from feeling down and despairing and back up to being happy and bubbly again. The truck driver was very friendly and we had quite a lengthy chat during the drive home. His name was Kenny, and he said it was usually quite lonely driving around all day with no-one to talk to. On finding out that my injury was due to a motorcycle crash, he said that he also had a motorbike as did his mates. Friendship sealed there and then. Most of his mates had bikes, mostly British ones, and it turned out that they often went to the same dances that I went to, and we had several mutual friends. He told me of some more venues where they would play a lot of rock and roll, and I wrote them down for future reference. I was really pleased as through adversity I now had another friend, and a whole new arena of evening entertainment had opened up. He said that many truck drivers were also motorcyclists, and that there was a certain kinship built up between bikers and truckers. Through the years bikers going to the many motorbike rallies and race meetings around the country, would often use the same transport cafes and inevitably would get talking with the lorry drivers. Also, the biking love of the open road instilling many of them into pursuing a driving career because of that.

Kenny gave me a few tips about road usage, and showed me how much more room trucks needed in order to get round some of the bends, and how roundabouts were the worst headache as a large truck would often need the whole of both lanes to manoeuvre around them. It helped to give me an appreciation that other road users had needs to be considered too. Even on that one journey several cars put themselves in danger by not allowing the truck room to move, and a couple nipped inside us on the roundabouts, and then bibbed indignantly on their hooters when the truck seemed to cut them off during the turn, unaware that they had moved into a 'blind' side as the truck made it's turn and squeezed them into the hedge, or worse still, onto the pavement area. I could see how stupid their actions were, and was quite glad to have seen this problem before I made the same mistake myself. Motorbike versus truck, only one outcome and it would not be the lorry that lost. This definitely highlighted the vulnerability of a motorbike to me, to be stored forever in my mind.

Mum was really surprised to see the truck pull up outside our house, and her face was a picture when I was lifted down out of the cab by my new friend. She wasn't too pleased when I told her I had hitched home, and she was very angry with the hospital for letting me go, but nothing could be done about it now, and it was partly her fault for not being there to answer my call earlier. Nothing could be done about it now, and I was home. She just had to make sure she was able to drive me to hospital for my next appointment.

Chapter 10

DOWN, BUT NOT OUT

I was beginning to feel sorry for Ben, as I knew it wasn't much fun to have a girlfriend who couldn't go out. He seemed to be very good about this though and said it wouldn't last forever. How true that turned out to be. Ben, whom I had now been going out with for nearly six months had managed to put my bike together again, using some parts from one of his own machines which was a similar model, but not in working form at that time. At least he was able to use my bike to come and visit me in the meantime. He still went to some of the dances on his own, on the pretext that he could tell me all about it when he came over, keeping me up to date with all the gossip etc. He said it would give him something to talk about. He forgot about the fact that everyone else was also keeping me updated. It didn't take long for the gossip to come home to roost. Ben had started seeing someone else, a girl called Janice. When I was first told that he seemed to be a bit particular about this girl I didn't believe it. I thought it was maybe an innocent friendship or a relation I did not know. However, as time wore on and he markedly didn't mention her name, I got suspicious and gradually gave credence to the rumours. It wasn't really the fact that he had found someone else, it happens, but the salt rubbed into the wound was that he was using my bike to take her out. This was not very easy to reconcile as it was a double piss take, firstly not to tell me he had someone else, and secondly to use my motorbike, I had to be sure before I made any accusations. I obviously had a big decision to make, and also I needed to have my bike back. Why is life never easy?

As I was still housebound unless someone was able to come and take me out, I had more than enough time to reflect on the situation as Ben was obviously diverted from his visits to me, which tailed off, and those he did make were shorter timespans too. The financial consideration was that he had my bike, and I needed that back. The emotional situation wasn't so straight forward. I was not prepared to share a boyfriend with anyone else, even if I cared about him. I knew I deserved better treatment than that. I wanted to tackle him and see whether he wanted us to still be together or not, but deep down, I knew I would never trust him again. I wasn't sure but didn't think so, and resigned myself to the fact that he would probably have to go. I didn't see much of Ben in the next few days, but I heard enough to make my blood boil.

First things first, it was more prudent to get the bike back. I asked Ben if he would leave the bike in the garage as my plaster cast was due to come off shortly, and I would need to start trying to ride it again. He didn't want to leave it at mine, as he felt that as he had put it back together again with a few parts from his bike and therefore it was now part his. I decided that this was not really fair, and I would have to get it back myself and be a bit devious about it. With this end in view, I developed a friend called John who might be able to help me. I would need a lift to get over to Ben's village in order to ride my bike back. This plan also necessitated the leg plaster to come off, so I had to wait another week.

I had it all thought out in my mind. The plaster would be coming off the following Wednesday, so I should be able to go over to collect my bike on the following weekend. I was totally unprepared for the shock when the plaster eventually came off. The muscles of my leg had atrophied and was only half the size of my left leg; in other words 'ceased up' due to lack of use. I was still unable to bend my leg more than about an inch. On questioning the doctor he informed me that it would take months before I could bend my leg normally. I was going to need extensive physiotherapy at the local community hospital to exercise it the right way to enable this. How bad can things get? Here I was thinking I could just get on with life, but no, more obstacles and time wasting. I was so upset, again the tears flowed. I guess at heart I am still quite emotional and not as tough as I thought. My mind raced with all sorts of wild thoughts; I might never get my bike back at this rate. Even worse than that, I might never be able to ride it again.

I was given an appointment for physiotherapy classes where I would relearn how to use my leg. I was not very enthusiastic as I had begun to think that I would never be right again. It seemed that my world had crumbled before I had had a chance to set it alight with my brilliance. However, my physiotherapist was really kind and patient, and after my first two sessions with her I perked up and got over my despondency. I worked hard at the exercises all day long. I determined to get my leg bending properly again. After constant working on it every day, I managed to get my leg bent enough within two weeks to go out on the back of John's motorbike, with my crutches poking into my boots to help me to hold them. John took me to the local Saturday night dance hall, which Ben had told me he didn't want to go to. Fate then took a hand to sort out my emotional life. We paid and went through the first set of doors, and then started to climb the flight of stairs to the ticket check doors, when half way up who should be coming back down the stairs, but Ben, complete with his new sidekick.

Ben looked stupidly astounded, and I couldn't hold my temper. I had a tantrum, there and then, with no more ado. The dance bouncer at the top door heard me, and was about to come down to see what the trouble was about, but just as he opened the door, I simultaneously dropped my crutches and swung my fist, catching Ben on the chin. The bouncer decided he did not want to get involved in a 'domestic' and backed off, shut his door, and held it so that we could not get in. Ben was taken aback, he clutched his chin which was bleeding by now, and started calling me all sorts of names. Rich as his new girlfriend stood there bemused as she did not know about me. I took advantage of this situation, and removed my bike keys from Ben's pocket and told him to keep away from me in future. John had by this time collected up my crutches and come up behind me, and promptly dragged me off in order to prevent any more disorder.

I was not much of a judge of boyfriends after all. John proved to be a good friend though, and after calming me down went back to talk to Ben about the bike. When Ben realised that I had known for a couple of weeks about his new girl, he was quite sheepish and sorry about the anguish he had caused me, not least deserting me when I was already in a bad state due to the accident. He was also anxious not to lose face with his mates about his behaviour towards me, especially as I was quite popular within his social group, John also made him see that a few parts did not give him any 'ownership' of my bike, and the use he had made of it for the previous few weeks was more than enough payback. John rode my bike home for me, immediately, and I got my stepfather to take us back to the dance. I thought, even if I am unable to ride it, I could always sell it and pay my stepfather back what I owed him.

When I finally got home again that night, it just got too much for me and yet again, I cried my eyes out. I went down into a dark state of self-pity for the next couple of weeks, feeling so hard done by that I felt as it I would never get over the whole episode. The crying and grief I felt was all mixed up and I didn't know whether it was for my dilapidated leg, my lost love or my damaged bike which I would now have to sell, most of all I had lost my self-esteem. Luckily, my optimistic personality saved me from total destruction. When I had got fed up sitting and feeling sorry for myself, my mind re-asserted itself and told me that my dejected state of mind would not last and life would still go on whether I joined in or not. I was a bit of a misery to be with during the next few weeks, but once I came to terms with myself I couldn't stay down forever. I'd survived, and I was about to enter the human race again with a vengeance. Never again would I cry over a bloke, they just weren't worth the effort. From now on it would be easy come, easy go. Just watch this space!

Chapter 11

GOING STRAIGHT

During my convalescence in the ensuing six months there was so much happening for me to really worry about any of the past unfortunate events. My parents were friendly with a very social group of people and my mother was always very enthusiastic with party going and throwing. If no-one had organised a party then it was a case of put names in a hat and whoever was drawn was the host for that night's event. If the weather was right, it may also be decided to have a party in the woods. Everyone would go home, ransack their fridges and freezers for foods, drinks and whatever else came to mind, and off everyone would go, complete with instruments for all to gather round and sing. It sounds crazy but was actually good fun, with a normal crowd of up to fifty people ready to have a good time.

As it was still extremely awkward for me to get around independently, several of mother's crowd would offer to take me along on some of these trips. This was my introduction to all-night parties, and an eye opener for me. My parent's parties were wilder than any of mine had been. No wonder most parents don't usually trust youngsters at parties, as they really do know what happens at them, and if they judge others on their own actions, which is normal process, then their antics were not very complimentary. Flirting was the order of the day, and hands on wherever possible. I felt quite prudish in comparison and usually sat with the musicians who seemed to me to be far safer to be near. I have never drunk alcohol and that alone was deemed a bit weird, even amongst my own friends. My parents group couldn't believe that I didn't indulge, but seeing the effects on otherwise rational people was not going to change my mind in that respect. Many was the time that I had to prop up my mum or my stepfather (often both at the same time) on our way home in the early hours.

Inevitably I developed a crush on one of the chaps in the group. He was very outgoing and according to my mum, a great guy. (What she meant was that he had a car and his own house). Anyway, we seemed to meet very regularly at this time, and as we got on very well we enjoyed a carefree flirtation. The romance was very lighthearted but fun, he wined while I had fruit juice as we dined and he taught me a lot about how not to take life too seriously; we had an enormous amount of fun that summer. He was one of the most happy fun-loving souls, despite being career conscious and in a good position workwise.

One of the funniest incidents during this period was when we had been at a long night party and did not notice the unexpected summer downpour. When we went to drive home that early morning, just after dawn, we opened the doors of his open topped sports car and promptly got our feet soaked as the water poured out onto our shoes from the flood within. He had left the roof down, and the car had semi filled with rainwater, ready to cascade over us. We both found this funny and cracked up laughing until we sat in the car, our clothes got absolutely soaked from sitting in the drenched seats. The upholstered seats worked like sponges and as soon as we sat in the car we both got a shock from the cold puddles we found ourselves in. The disaster was completed when we got home to mine and found the house locked and I had no key. The parents were still not home, and no telling how long they would be, or where they were as they had not been at our party. Nothing for it but to go back to his place. We showered in order to warm up again, I borrowed a dressing gown and he put our clothes in the washing machine. We drank coffee and talked and talked, and having no idea when the parents would get home I stayed the night. We then slept until about lunchtime whereupon he cooked me a great English breakfast before running me home. Again, although the door was now open there was still nobody home, so after leaving a note to say where I was (not that anyone would care) we went shopping in the City. The car had mostly dried out as it was a lovely hot day, but a couple of bin bags on the seats was all that was needed and off we went.

We drove up to town in his car, with the hood still down, having a good time just enjoying each other's company. It was nice to feel wanted again after my recent disaster and was a great tonic for my confidence. The first thing we did was to go to a couple of motoring shops as my friend wanted to get some plugs and things in order to give his car a service. Once the essentials had been purchased we went round the shops to pass the time. As is usual when shopping, I couldn't resist popping into a couple of clothes shops, and once there I found a few bargains and just had to try some on. Having a man around while buying a few items of clothing suddenly seemed odd. It was definitely a new experience as normally only mother or sisters had ever shopped with me before. This was a feminine side of me which I had not really considered to exist before, at least, not existed for me, or so I had thought. Maybe we do all have this need for flattery, but it was great after my deflated ego of the past few months. This realisation of my femininity and of enjoying his approval of my choices was thought provoking to say the least. There was a curious intimacy in this action and it made me feel more mature and worldly wise. The day was rounded off very neatly with my man suggesting lunch at The Mill on our way back home. The day had been very spontaneous, unexpectedly pleasant, totally unplanned but cosy, friendly, romantic and intimate without being intrusive or pressured. This gave me a lot to think about and showed me another side to life, feelings and how good it was to be treated in a considerate and appreciative way. The mood was to live for the moment and enjoy what you are doing, as you do it.

During the spring and summer the weather was mostly good and we were never short of parties, dances and barbecues to go to. Many of the parties would last until dawn, at least. There were many memorable moments but one of the most awkward events was after a particularly riotous all-nighter at a friend's house. It had been just another one of those spontaneous affairs, and Craig and I had followed the crowd, joining in all the fun wholeheartedly. Michael was the host this time, and he had recently had a blazing row with his regular girlfriend and was feeling despondent. During the party he flirted quite outrageously with my friend Angela. We had all had a really good time and by the time the party had finished, it was already dawn and even the diehards had straggled their way home, Craig and I had already commandeered the spare room, both chaps having had too much drink to drive Angela so she had also decided to stay the night too. We tumbled through to the various bedrooms and fell asleep.

By early lunchtime that next day, Michael's former girlfriend, Sara, had heard about the party and came round. She was furious at not having been invited, and hammered on the door. Michael came through to our room, woke Craig up and said it was his girlfriend. He wanted us to cover for him because Angela was still there, and he didn't want to have another row in the state he was in. Craig and I hurriedly went to the door, having grabbed a couple of towels in our rush to cover our modesty. When we answered the door, Sara stormed past us into the kitchen, ranting and raving about not being told about the party and demanding to know where Michael was. At this point, Angela came wandering into the kitchen, looking as bleary eyed as we felt, and dressed in a skimpy hand towel which barely covered anything. Sara rounded on her and in order to stop a fight, Craig intervened by putting his arm around Angela and blocking Sara's path, swearing blind that she was with him. Sara then swung round to me, knowing that I had been seeing Craig and asked who had I been with then? Having been put in this awkward corner, I replied that I too had been with Craig, whereupon he put his arm around me too and swore that we were both with him. The three of us, pathetically wrapped in towels, trying to look unphased by the interrogation.

Sara stormed past us demanding again to know where Michael was. Craig, trying to think more clearly said that he was sure that Daniel had driven him home during the night when Michael had got worse for wear. Poor Sara! Screaming back at us she reminded us that we were in Michael's house and he would not need to go home. Upon Craig's reply that he must have forgotten that in his stupor, and her own fruitless search of the bedrooms seemed to bear this absence up, she had to be contented with this, so she then left us and went off to Daniel's place in search of her Michael. This left us wondering where on earth Michael had got to. A thorough search of the house failed to reveal Michael, and we had no idea where he could have gone. We quickly raced around getting some clothes on, then went outside to search for him. At first we could not see him, however, looking up we soon saw him, up in the boughs and peeping over the arms of a large old oak tree – beautifully clad in a flowing white sheet. All he needed was a pair of small white wings and he could almost have passed for a cherub – although the moustache and long black beard spoiled the effect.

Over the summer Craig and I had many good times together, and although we had many common interests and friends, we also had several different likes and dislikes. Our general friendship went well and was what I needed at that time. The fact that Craig had a car made it easier for me to get about as my leg was still not quite right and although no longer needing sticks, it would not have held up to enable me to have another motorbike quite yet. The best thing about Craig's car was that it was an open top sports car, an MG Midget, so it was almost like being on a bike with loads of windy fresh air. I learnt about the merits of various cars and reading up in some of Craig's motoring magazines I found that although there was a lot more to them, basically they had the same technicalities as motorcycles. I easily kept up with the menfolk and their car talk, again surprising some of them when they realised that I understood much of their conversation. The only difference was that I wasn't as interested in their version of makes and models as I had been in the two-wheeled equivalents. I was getting to be a confirmed petrol head by this time, and my interest in cars did start to manifest itself.

I had still kept in touch with my biking friends as I fully intended to keep riding, whatever my new friends thought. I might be growing up, but I wasn't yet ready to go straight. All night parties and hellraising were all right in their way, but give me good old foot stomping, rhythm and jiving, rock and roll. The passion for folk music and banjo playing amongst the older set was not really my scene, and although enjoyable in its own way, in my opinion did not match and could not compete with the vibrancy of real live groups and bands. As my leg grew in strength, and I regained a bit more of my earlier independence and confidence, I slowly spent more time with my biking mates. My leg was now well and truly on the mend, and so was I. I kept in touch with the older group and with Craig, but we were basically very different people, and as much as the fling had done a lot to restore my character back to normal, it was never a long-lasting type of relationship. Craig had also given me an ultimatum to choose between him and two wheels (which he considered dangerous) and so we parted company. The friendship had been good for me at the time, but, although fun, the sports car could not survive the pull of the motorcycle season. Many of my mates gradually started to go off to more and more motorcycle race meetings around the country, I wanted to go too, and did.

Chapter 12

TRY AND TRY AGAIN

My circle of friends was just getting wider and wider all the time. I often saw my trucker friend, Kenny, and got to know many of his friends. One of them was quite nice and started asking me out, especially when he realised I actually liked motorbikes enough to have bought my own. The only thing that spoilt him in my eyes was his inability to buy a girl anything less than Southern Comfort. He said he was too embarrassed to ask for a Coke. Other than that he seemed OK, and more importantly in my eyes when I learned he had a Norton Commando – one of the most iconic British bikes at the time. I definitely wanted to have a go on that and I soon wangled a ride. Brian was intending to go to Brands Hatch to watch a motorcycle Grand Prix. I had never been to a motorcycle race meeting before and decided I had to go. I offered to share petrol costs if he would take me and this was agreed to. He would pick me up on the Sunday at 7 o'clock in the morning. I was all set to have a good time, and no-one was going to stop me. Not even the weather. We set off, but by the time we got halfway there the rains started. It rained all the rest of the way there, all the time we were there, and all of the way home again. From about half past eight in the morning to half past nine in the evening it rained. The deluge did not dampen my spirits though.

That is when I finally realised that I had truly flipped my lid, as I really had enjoyed my whole day. Brian thought I was mad but loved it, for a girl to ride pillion on a bike without complaining or moaning about something was quite a novelty for him. Not only that, but to be soaked for the better part of the day and evening and still not moan about his beloved motorbike was unheard of. He was smitten. For me, the sound as we rode up and while we were parking was absolutely enlivening. I heard a really deep throated Rah-ooom….. Rah-ooom rrrrrrr …... Rah-ooom….. Rah-ooom of a bike being revved up, then purring, then revved up again, the sound reverberated in the open air almost as if it was in an enclosed space. Brian told me this was the iconic MV Augusta and that his idol Phil Read would be riding it. I must admit the sound was gut-stirring and so recognisable when being prepped for the racing by the team mechanics. This was indelible, etched in my sound memory banks forever.

That particular meeting was the one where they raced the opposite way around the circuit to usual, and there were many spills and tumbles on the track due to the wet surface. Luckily none were serious. The highlight of my day was when the two factory Nortons came first and second in the main race, about a lap and a half ahead of the others. The rider's names were Peter Williams and Dave Croxford, and their bikes made the most incredible sound as they went around the track together. They just thumped their way round from start to finish, and no-one seemed able to keep with them. This increased my pleasure knowing that I was riding (albeit pillion) on a bike like theirs, and made me feel like a queen for the day. This was the first of many Grand Prix trips for me, and I was thoroughly hooked.

The second trip that Brian took me to was the Grand Prix at Silverstone. We arrived and as it was a much sunnier day had plenty of time to look around the many stands and stalls scattered around the circuit. Even though we were not going to buy much as there wasn't any room on the bike to carry stuff, we enjoyed window shopping. One of the more memorable stands was the Laverda show stand, displaying their new Jota 1000 which was being launched. All eager to see whether I could aspire to one of these gleaming red/orange hunks of metal, I scrambled aboard the exhibit – horrifying Brian, who promptly tried to disengage from ever knowing me – and the poor salesman panicking in case I dislodged the bike from its stand. To this day I can see the look of terror on the poor man's face, eyes almost bulging as he raced to hold the bike steady and help me off his precious charge. It was an extremely tall bike, and I obviously could not reach the floor, even on tip toes, so I crossed the Laverda off my list of possible future possessions and got off, to the intense relief of the Laverda Rep. Still, there were many more makes in the sea at that time, so I gaily thanked the chap for his help, and made my way around to more suitable trade stands. There was always something inevitable about me and two wheels, and again I felt an incredible urge to have another bike of my own.

There were many good dances around and my new friends would jive and bop all night long. This music was so alive and I just could not stop myself from joining in and letting my hair down. My mates and I would still go dancing three or four times a week. Although I had been dating Brian for a few weeks, we did not really suit very well and we agreed mutually to keep it as friends only, and I was free to do my own thing. I was attracted to another lad in the group, I started spending a bit of time with Stu who was closer to me in age and mentality, and he had a Triumph 650cc TR6. Stu had another big bonus in that like me, he did not smoke which made a refreshing change as nearly everyone I knew smoked, and I hated it. In those days smoking was the norm and you were considered strange if you didn't participate in this pastime. The other good thing about Stu was that he was in a mechanical apprenticeship at the time. He was more than happy to buy a Coke for me when we went out, and that took the pressure off of me to drink alcohol. We had a great relationship, learning to jive together and when not dancing about, we spent our time listening to music. Rock and Roll of course. We drove Stu's parents mad when we decided to learn the words, and we spent many hours together, writing down the words to all our favorite records and tapes, but it got worse when we started to sing (croon, or screech) along to the tracks. Stu's dad started singing 'all I want for Christmas is a pair of ear muffs"!

Stu was doing a day release scheme for his work at the local college and sometimes I would meet him after college and we would go straight out from there. On one such occasion I was looking amongst the motorcycles for Stu's machine when I noticed a 'For Sale' notice on one. I took a closer look at it, and it was a really pretty little machine which I immediately took a fancy to. Excitedly, I raced to find Stu and asked him to give me his opinion to see if he thought it might suit me. He approved of my choice and I stayed by the little bike until the owner appeared. We agreed a price of £90.00 and I paid a deposit of £10.00 there and then. We exchanged telephone numbers and addresses, and the lad agreed to give me a week to raise the rest of the money and to arrange for its collection. He lived about eight miles out the other side of the city. I was very apprehensive about riding again this time though, so Stu rode it home for me. Stu's mother took us there in her Mini. I was now the proud owner of a BSA Bantam. The model was a D14/4 Bushman and it was only about 4 years old. I hoped that I would have more luck this time.

However, things were very different. Stu was fully aware of my accident and would not let me go out on my new bike until he had shown me how to service the bike and I could prove that I could start it easily. The motorcycle was a two-stroke and being more modern than the James, was much easier to kick start – it did not have an electric start but was so light and easy that was not a problem. Once Stu was satisfied that I was competent with the workings of my Bantam, and could trouble-shoot and do minor fault finding and get-me-home repairs, he let me go out for a ride.

My first venture out on it started one Sunday morning and I enjoyed being out and about so much I went practically to all the corners of the county. I rode well over a hundred miles that day, but when I eventually got back I was more than happy with my new purchase. It was such an easy machine to both start and ride, and as it was not very fast I built up my confidence without going overboard. This was one of the best times of my life and everything seemed to go well again for me. Stu was also very good for me, while teaching me a lot about the actual mechanics of motorcycles and insisted that if I was going to ride a bike I had better learn fully how they work, not just know how to, but to do it too.

To this end, if anything needed doing to either his or my motorcycle he made sure that any work was done when I could be there to either help him, or to do it with his supervision. He would help me do as much of the work as possible, with his guidance, only helping if I could not physically undo any fixings through lack of strength. I was finally realising my ambition of being a mechanic. I was especially proud when I managed to open up the clutch section, take out and inspect the clutch plates and replace the worn ones. Even better when Stu took it for a test ride afterwards and pronounced it as working perfectly, even though the brains had been his own, I had done it. It was great to be treated as an equal in this way despite my hands ending up blacker than Stu's.

Stu had been saving up to get a newer bike for quite some time now and was hoping to get a Norton Commando, like many of our friends had. I was pleased to think about getting another bike and together we started looking around to see what prices they were making. We looked in the local paper, and in the national motorcycle magazines. We went to see several bikes in the area, but most seemed quite expensive compared to the prices in the specialised rags. We advertised the Triumph to see what sort of price we could get for that. Several people came to look and in the end we made a deal with a chap about our age. He was very keen as Stu had maintained it in really good order and he gave us a better price than we had expected. Stu took a large deposit and we then had three days to find ourselves a Norton.

We rang up, visited and dismissed a couple of bikes locally and decided to look further afield. Looking in the national magazines and papers we decided to go to London and found a few dealerships to go and have a look at. There were a couple of bike shops on Leytonstone High Road as we rode into London, but we didn't find anything suitable, the bikes themselves were mainly in a poor state of neglect and not what we expected. We carried on into the middle of the City, eventually finding Pride and Clarkes near the Elephant and Castle I believe. Again, although the bikes were maybe presented better we found we were not that impressed with the bikes offered, and the prices seemed a bit over the top. We decided to cut our losses and go home without buying anything.

We were a bit despondent that evening and although it was a bit later than we would normally go to the pub we decided to go for a quick drink to mull things over. Brian was in there and we got talking about our trip to the smoke. To our surprise Brian laughed, quite insensitively I thought, considering our sad state of affairs. He then said that he was going to sell his bike and was going to get a brand-new Ducati. He had been planning to keep it quiet and surprise everyone as he was going to trade in his Norton with the dealer. He said if we were interested we were welcome to match the price offered by the dealer, ie trade value, which proved to be a great price for us. Stu jumped at the chance as he knew the bike's complete history as Brian had had it from new, and like Stu, had looked after it properly and had a complete main dealer service history. Brian was pleased to think his bike was going to a home where he knew it would be looked after well, and we were happy as we paid a good price for an exceptional bike.

This started us on a thoroughly brilliant and enjoyable year of touring and camping around the country. Have bike, will travel. We went to most of the Race meetings in the southern half of England including Brands Hatch, Silverstone, Mallory Park, Snetterton and Cadwell Park. During the latter part of the summer we even ventured taking a holiday down in Hampshire near my grandmother's house at Fording bridge. This was not far from Salisbury and the plan was to go to a race meeting at Truxton where they had an enduro race. This meeting was for a 400 mile race but we both found this one a bit boring as we couldn't keep up with who was on which lap, so it was confusing as to who was actually winning or not. Still, it was interesting even if it was a meeting we would not repeat in a hurry. We decided that short circuit racing was more watchable and kept to the more usual meetings after that.

We also sampled the action and vibrancy of a few scrambles meetings at Cadder's Hill in Norfolk. I can remember that this event was regularly televised in the 1950s and early 1960s, and vividly recall my father watching it on a small black and white TV in the living room. Cadder's Hill was then a major national meeting and still hosts regular events over seventy years on from then. The start was something incredible to watch, as sometimes up to fifty bikes would line up at the starting line, waiting for the gun to fire. Once fired they would all just go full pelt into the first 'target' of a gap in the fence only about six yards wide. The race was not on their minds, only getting to that gap before all the other lads, because if they didn't get there within the first ten bikes, it was almost guaranteed they would get caught up in a melee of bikes jammed together and if you were unfortunate enough to sustain breakages in that scrum, then your race was over before it had started. Once through that narrow opening, it was full pelt up one of the steepest hills in Norfolk, and then winding in and around a snaking track up and down that hill, to eventually do the steepest climb before going 'over the top'. This was so steep that most of the bikes would do a leap off the top to hopefully land upright before careering down a sandy hill, offering no traction, just soft sand to try to ride through without falling off, or being landed on by riders who were behind you, then going through a small gap abreast of the original starting line to then filter back up and around the track again. There were many inroads where the spectators could get to in order to see the racing from different vantage points, and close enough to get some beautiful photos of the various competitors. This was a fantastic spectator sport for all, as it was normal for us to be able to mingle within the 'pits' and to be able to interact with the riders, many of whom were biker-hold revered names.

This summer we had acquired ourselves a really strong ridge tent, and we took full advantage of a warm summer; camping overnight at most of these race meetings. I was also instructed in the correct way to put a tent up, first of all necessities was to work out the way the land sloped as it was unusual to have a lovely flat area for camping. The main reason for this is that you need to have your entrance at the lower end, because if it rained in the night, the water would then roll downhill, and not funnel into the tent for your early morning (or midnight) wash. Great tip that, as we often saw novices fall foul of this and hear their screams and shouts when so rudely awakened. The next thing was to check the area for stones, especially sharp ones, as the last thing you want in the night is to wake up with a sore back where you had lain on a stone underneath the groundsheet, especially if said ground sheet was integral to the tent itself, as the tent would have to be taken down again in order to find and remove the offending stone. If one had been sensible enough to actually take an airbed – contentious when the controller was intent on saving weight on his precious machine – but essential for a better night's sleep when 'roughing' it. Once we were happy with the basic preparation, then comes the laying out of the tent, and putting it up properly stretched. Ridge tents usually had the inner tent, and if not stretched properly and the pole spacers arranged on top of the inner ridge ends, then it was necessary to put the rain cover over the top, making sure again that it was stretched properly so that it did not touch the more delicate inner tent. Why? Because if the outer skin touched the inner skin, if it rained, the water would again cause a problem as it would seep through the non-waterproof inner skin and yes, you've got it, we would have an early morning wash again, but at least if your tent was properly sited with heads uphill it might only be your bottom half that got soaked. This scenario would of course be offset by my beloved airbed, unless one was unlucky enough to have turned over and was hugging the inner tent, in which case the drenching was obligatory.

This was obviously not the end of the 'correct way' to set up camp. The outer tent had to be pegged down properly, with the pegs angled in towards the tent at the bottom, so the ropes did not inadvertently pull the pegs out during the night. Once the ordinary outer sheet was pegged down, there was the extra security of the storm lines required. This meant stronger ropes being thrown over, criss cross fashion – don't ask – four ways and again, pegged down with industrial size tent pegs. I thought he didn't want to carry too much weight!

Having camped the night before the racing we then had a relaxed early start at the event. We would normally pay the extra for a ticket to allow us into the pits, where we would spend hours looking at the various team machines, looking for their ingenious solutions to various problems, seeing new innovations and being amused at some of the crazy 'bodge' jobs that some of the mechanics would apply, to hopefully get their steeds through the next race as there was not facilities for proper repairs mid pre-race prepping. It used to be very educational, especially so as Stu was technical enough to work out what had been done, information always stored as some of these unorthodox resolutions to problems might be a life-saver if one broke down in a rural area, and could perhaps get you home.

The other thing I took from all this university of life education was, it was an eye-opener for what you could keep in your road tool kit. I always try to keep a bit of insulating tape, a couple of paper clips, a bit of string, old ten pence coin, alongside the basic screwdriver, phillips, set of allen keys, small adjustable spanner and hammer either in my car or on my bikes. I did used to keep the same tools in my handbag, but when I weighed it once and saw I was carrying around almost three kilo of excess weight in my bag, I decided that was a bit excessive, my shoulder was more useful for hanging my arms on. I ended up having a really good weather proof wax cotton jacket which had really useful pockets and that sufficed me from then on. The bonus for this was that I no longer needed a handbag, as there were plenty of pockets for everything.

Back to the camping, and it was interesting to see the variety of facilities at the different sites. Here I have to compliment Snetterton circuit because toilet facilities were often an afterthought during those years, but Snetterton had built several properly plumbed-in toilet/washing facilities around the race track, and camping areas, so it was very civilised. They also seemed to realise that to provide enough facilities for the ladies – as many were dragged reluctantly along by their enthused men-folk – so I guess this was their way of trying to make it easier on the men to provide some comfort for the women. They also realised that for thousands of spectators it was imperative for enough female accommodation – the simple fact of life is that women do have other things pressing against their bladders and need facilities more frequently than their chaps. And, when we need to go, we need to go, NOW. We do not have the dubious pleasure of being able to air it without serious gravity and modesty issues. If any event organisers are reading this, take note. Also, as we need to powder our noses at the same time, we tend to take more time, and getting through our various warmth inducing layers of clothing means our visits are also generally more time consuming. Again, this is one occasion where more is definitely more.

One of the funniest things I remember (after initial annoyance) is one weekend at Mallory Park, we had arrived early on the Friday for an all weekender as we had thought it would be good to see the practice sessions on the Saturday. Having set up, gone into town for a meal and drink we came back and were looking forward to a peaceful night. However, during the night one inebriated person had decided to have a lark about and started up a fairly small two-stroke bike. It had a very tinny screeching high-pitched sound, but the rider proceeded to annoy several of the campers by riding around the campsite, deliberately trying to wake most of us up. The noise of the motorbike in itself was an irritation, and several people started voicing their anger and shouting from the many tents. I was on the point of going out and having a few choice words myself; before it had a chance to get nasty however, it all rebounded back on the idiotish rider when, for all to hear, his engine backfired and sounded as though it had blown up. The resulting silence was deadly. Suddenly a tremendous roar went up all around the campsite as people cheered and clapped at this welcome finale. I guess the offending chap must have slunk off, hopefully totally embarrassed at the resounding appreciation of the ignoble finish. The clapping and cheering went on for about ten minutes then settled down, and the rest of the weekend went well for most of us.

Chapter 13

FUN AND FRIENDSHIPS

My circle of friends had grown ever larger over time, and I had actually accumulated several different groups of mates in slightly different geographical areas as my own ability to 'go here, go there, go anywhere' increased. The souls who had first joined in the adventures on the railway trolley and café scene were one group; then I had the early moped group which initially sparked my two wheel interest. I had the older folk and woodland party group during my convalescence, and then there was the early 'teach me to ride groups', leading last but not least to my dance hall groups. Alongside all these social groups were also various essential groups, as in workplace groups, shopping groups and people I got to know as I wandered around the town I called home. If you sit down and think about the number of people you can get to know in just a couple of years, it is staggering. From moving to the town at the age of 16 to my early independence and subsequent forays around my area, I had gathered quite a large list of friends, family, more friends and then the acquaintances we start gathering, as we roll like leaves blowing in the wind through our later teen lives.

The dance halls were important to me. The lads Stu and I hung around with became some of the best friends who have stood the test of time. There was a great core of about a dozen mates who mostly lived in the one village, padded out with a few of their likeminded workmates who regularly joined us in our various adventures and nights out. Stu and I spent a lot of time with Stu's mate Danny who ended up dating one of my friends, Susan. Susan and myself lived about 20 miles away from Stu and Danny's village so it quickly became a routine for the boys to ride over together to see Susan and I about four times a week, namely Wednesday and Friday nights, then Saturday afternoon and evenings with Sunday evening completing the week's entertainment. Sometimes Susan and I would pal up and go to the dance halls on the courtesy buses which saved the lads some time and fuel but it was great to have them take us home. The boys were both really good company, with good jobs and making their way in life. They had really friendly open natures and likewise their mates were similarly inclusive and made us girls feel part of them.

There was a lovely family of three brothers Mav (a short form of his nickname, Maverick – presumably after a popular cowboy on TV) and his two younger brothers. Mav had a really beautiful old Vincent Thousand which was considered the Rolls Royce of bikes; his brothers both had beautiful gleaming Nortons. Bob had a bright red 750cc Roadster and Neil had a large black Interstate. All this group spent many hours in their workshops polishing and cleaning, maintaining and just enjoying their iconic bikes. The brothers lived close by to Brian who had the Norton 750cc Fastback in a very distinctive sparkly orange colour. Danny had just acquired his Norton Roadster which was a beautiful mid blue colour – and my Stu had his 650cc Triumph until we bought Brian's Fastback Norton and Brian progressed to his beloved Ducati 900 Desmo Duke. I was in heaven. The brothers had a great cousin, David who had a Triumph 5TA. David was a lovely larger than life character who overshadowed his bike considerably. All the lads in this group made Susan and I totally included, their manners were lovely and they all had kind attitudes and the camaraderie they fostered was warm and inviting. Some of the workmates who lived elsewhere and invariably extended our social events or ride outs were Knotty with his Norvin which he had sprayed with a small picture and sign written Armageddon on the tank – anyone from those days may remember the magazine character this honoured. He was besotted with his bike, and it only came out on high days or holidays. Another great mate worked as an engineer and had a fantastic old Norton Dominator 650ss which he had bought as a 'bitsa' (basically a box of parts, supposedly a complete bike) and lovingly rebuilt this into a much-admired café racer with clip-ons and rear-pegs as per the fashion at this time.

It is humbling to think that 50 years on I still count this group of lads as friends, and we often see each other at 'bike nights' around the county, even though we now range in age from 60ish to 80ish. The greetings are always hugs and smiles with the ease of many years of joint adventures and memories. As with many motorcycle groups, the friendships forged all those years ago have endured and thrived – contacts still strong and bonded together through the love of bikes. We may sometimes go a few years without seeing each other, but as soon as we glimpse each other across a village green, or playing field at shows, it is as if we have never been apart. The biking community is one of the strongest of social bonded groups I have ever encountered, who encompass all and sundry from all walks of life, and all come together without judgement to just enjoy the company of likeminded souls.

The dance halls were the highlight of our weekends, and our music was mainly rock and roll, closely followed by the contemporary sounds of glam rock. The most exciting for me was the rock and roll, and seeing the couples jiving was inspiring to us younger teenagers. Our mate Mav was one of the older lads in our circle and he could jive really well. Susan and I decided to ask if he would teach us which he agreed to, and being a really good natured chap he kept his word. The first step was to learn to 'bop' in order to get and understand the basic rhythms of the music, synchronising to the bouncy actions. With that sorted, Mav then showed us each part of the dance bit by bit, repeating each part before going to slightly different repetitions. It was exhilarating when our lessons culminated in Mav dancing with both Susan and I at the same time, holding each of us in different hands at the same time, with us doing our routines in sync. We really felt that we had arrived.

Over a few months we danced with him to the point where we were confident enough to in turn pass these skills to our lads, Stu and Danny. The ability to dance properly with a partner greatly enhanced our enjoyment not just then, but throughout our lives, and I have noticed ever since that couples who dance together usually stick together. Many of our friends are still in the same relationships having fun together, still enjoying their lives together. As more of us danced regularly, we were never short of partners as the whole group was friendly and lively. This was a particularly great group to be with making us feel a part of something alive and vibrant. It gave us more than enough to while away our time, and although the 'Biker' or 'Greebo' labels which society as a whole ascribed to us in a none too friendly way at that time, we were happily occupied and did not have time to interfere or annoy anyone else who was not within our spheres. There was rivalry between groups, but never really any animosity as we were having too much fun to really even notice those with different opinions. Each to their own. We appreciated that not everyone wanted to conform to 'society', so why should others need to 'conform' to what we wanted to do. There was a culture of tolerance, the only criteria to being integrated with us was the common love of motorbikes, and dancing.

During this time we saw many talented local bands, doing covers of our various icons, as in Elvis, Eddie Cochran, Billy Fury, Gene Vincent, Bill Haley, Buddy Holly, Jerry Lee Lewis, Little Richard, Big Boppa, Cliff Richard and the Shadows... There were so many oldies, and also many up and coming artists, some following the traditional sounds with their own music like Status Quo, Suzie Quatro, Sweet, T-Rex and Slade among many others in the Glam Rock era. I remember Screaming Lord Sutch coming up behind me at one venue, putting his outsized grizzly hand on my shoulder expecting me to jump out of my skin, but as I had always been in the thick of things, usually being the butt of the joke, I didn't even flinch. This turned the tables on this crazy artist, but we had a little joke before he went up on stage to perform his funereal show. Very dark but so entertaining. I also remember seeing Golden Earring when they came over from Europe to play. They had so many speakers and apparatus the stage was too small, so all we could see was the top of their heads, and almost hear the sound. I ended up going outside and sitting on the clifftop half a mile away, where I could hear them perfectly; but to be inside the hall there was so noisy, it was difficult to hear the group: Overkill on the ears.

We had many ride outs and explored much of our county during our busy weekends. We would go in various size packs to the coast, mooch about, eat burgers and hot dogs, ice-creams etc. My bike was considerably slower than the lads Nortons so mostly I rode pillion behind Stu for these outings, but I would commute to work on my bike, and often take myself shopping on a Saturday morning in order to get practice on my little Bantam. I was clocking up the miles and gaining in confidence all the time. One such trip into the city resulted in yet another friendship when I had decided to go home. Riding from the city, I had got about two miles from the city centre when I saw a chap with a crash helmet on his arm, hitch-hiking beside the road. There was quite a bit of anti-biker phobia at this time, and I thought the poor chap would probably have a problem getting a lift. However, I had often been grateful for lifts and felt this time I could repay the favour, albeit to a different recipient, so I stopped and offered my pillion seat. The poor chap was a bit astounded as my motorcycle was rather small, and he was probably about double my size – I was only about seven stone in weight – but it was a case of 'Hobson's choice' so after making sure that he did actually need to go close to my destination, and had passed his test, so I was okay taking him on the back, he got on the back of my Bantam. The little motorcycle was rather overloaded, and struggled valiantly with this extra burden, and I dropped my new friend off in his village. This was an extra four miles but I acquired a new friend, Guy (Big G), who turned out to be a rock and roll DJ – result. Yet another avenue for entertainment, he told me where he would often be playing in certain local pubs.

Another memorable trip which Stu, Danny, Susan and I went on was when we had been shopping together in the city, and the local motorcycle shop we habitually went to was putting on a coach trip to Meriden, the home of the Triumph Motorcycle. This looked interesting, and Stu was keen to go to see how the factory operated, and how the iconic motorcycles were made. It was an opportunity not to be missed. We all bought tickets and eagerly awaited the day.

Again, it was an early start, I believe we had to be up about 4:30 in the morning in order to get to the bike shop for pick-up at 6am. We all arrived and excitedly got on the bus when it arrived. The trip was almost fully subscribed, and set off only about 15 minutes behind schedule: The four of us chatting and looking forward to the day ahead. As was usual then, we stopped at another favourite transport café, between Guyhirn and Thorney on the A47. We all dived in for a full breakfast, chatted within our groups and with some of the lorry drivers who were interested in where we were off to.

The journey onward was still cheerful although seemed to take a long time to get there. On arrival we were all checked into the factory tour, with an initial talk from one of the designated managers who went through the rules of behaviour on the factory floor. First there was an overview of emergency and first aid procedures. We had to be aware that this is a workplace, with many dangerous pieces of equipment and machinery around the place. Also we had to be careful as many forklifts and trolleys were moving around the benches. Basically, we were to avoid getting in the way of operations, as we went around viewing the various work stations. We were lucky enough to have one of the research and development engineers talk to us about how the designers had their various ideas developed, and how Triumph had come up with an ingenious 'modular' design approach for the future, but they were not hopeful of it being taken forward. This seemed to me to be sad, as the whole idea was to cut down on the variety of spares as the components were to be standardised to incorporate many interchangeable parts. The worldwide industry seems to have gone the other way instead, with many bikes since using different parts within the same year, to the point where you have to know not just what year the bike was produced, but almost down to what month it was made. This latter approach making bikes practically obsolete within months of their production.

After the informative sessions, we were then let loose to watch proceedings, and what a hive of activity it was. We were separated into about four groups of a dozen each, in order to be less obtrusive as we were shown around. It was spellbinding to see the craftmanship of the various employees, many of whom were motorcyclists themselves. As I remember there were sections where parts were built up on benches, but then the assemblers had responsibility of building the bikes up totally from their component parts. They would get the frames, wheels and forks from the main area in order to build up a rolling chassis, then obtain the bits and bobs from around the factory and put it all together. Each man responsible for the bike he was working on. The speed which these boys could assemble a bike was amazing, and I wished I worked close enough to have been a part of it, however, I did not see any women working there so perhaps they may not have wanted me. One of the most fascinating jobs was the 'paint shop' men. To watch as they sprayed the tanks and mudguards was fascinating, but the real craftsmanship was the elite painters who did the decal work – painting the lines and other insignia – all by hand and by eye. They were outstanding in their workmanship, needing the most steady hands to paint fine or thick lines alongside each other, leaving delineations accurately between these lines. They were so talented, and unsung. Another enduring memory from that trip was their stores re-order system, which was basically a double or triple line of parts bins, when the bin in front was empty, it was removed and the parts re-ordered whilst the workers then used the second or third bin. Easy, simple, and visible stock control.

The trip home on the bus, with the obligatory evening meal at the Thorney Cafe, was animated as everyone wanted to recount their favourite sections of the factory. Stu was entranced by the whole event and had taken ideas home for practice. Little did we know that it would only be a few years after that when Meriden shut down and the history was obliterated. Such a shame and when this happened I could only look back in sadness at all those dedicated workers being put aside by the short-sightedness of the powers that were in charge at the time. One of my later friends recounted the dejected atmosphere when he went to collect a bike he had ordered and paid for. He turned up after working abroad with the intention of collecting his bike, to find that it was the penultimate Triumph to leave the factory, only one other left for someone to collect. He was lucky as if he had been delayed on his return to England, he may not have been able to collect it at all. He did feel there was an atmosphere of sadness around the site where once it had been such a hive of positive activity.

Chapter 14

THE STEAM RACKET COMPANY

Stu, Danny, Susan and I decided to go on holiday together, and the only place we considered at that time was, 'The Isle of Man'. This small island nestled between England, Scotland, Wales and Ireland was the only objective to be thought of. The famous Motorcycle road race circuit – *and we had it here* – in our own country. There was no-where else that drew our attention, and amongst our friends if you liked motorcycles it was a '*must go*' holiday. So many of the older friends had been, not just once but many times. The racing had started in 1907 continuously apart from the two world wars, and had a special place in the hearts of motorcycle enthusiasts around the world. Most top names were nobody if they had not raced there. The well-known names from John Surtees, Agostini, Phil Read, most of all Mike 'the bike' Hailwood. Also, George Formby in his absolutely hilarious film 'No Limits' which was a cinematic '*must see*' opportunity whilst visiting this beautiful island. We read and studied all we could in the national motorbike magazines and papers for any information we could.

The four of us started planning our trip, spending hours together plotting the route to Liverpool, booking the Bed & Breakfast accommodation. Unfortunately as we had not started looking until January, much of the accommodation was already fully booked, and so we were unable to book into the same premises. However, at least we were within a mile of each other in Douglas, the main town and where it all happened, but being young and fit that was fine. The boats were on a first come, first serve basis so that did not appear to be a problem, we would get there and buy our tickets before embarking on the appropriate boats.

There was a lot of preparing to do, not least for Susan and I to have appropriate long distance motorcycle gear. To this end we decided to have a day shopping in order to see what was about, and what we would need to spend. We went up to the city of Norwich where we had about four motorbike shops to look around. At that time, there were three main shops and another more eccentric chap who ran a shop where, if he didn't like you, you were not allowed in, whatsoever. If he let you in, you were honoured if he let you buy anything. Every visit you would be scrutinised to check if he had time to be bothered with you. He was very well-known and to be allowed into his hallowed grounds was the ambition of most of our contemporaries. A visit into his workshop was something to be proud of, like a badge of honour. Ever since I turned up on my Bantam, needing to borrow a spanner one day, he had seemed to like me so we did have the chance to peep around for a short while. He obviously knew Stu as well, so they chatted mechanics for a while.

Jeff did not have any motorcycle clothing for sale, so after looking at a Norton Hi-rider Commando we left and went to the other shops for a browsing session. We ended up at Tinkler's which was in a back street in the city, but was peopled by ordinary bikers and Stu insisted that I spend my hard-earned monies on a Belstaff one-piece waxed-cotton waterproof suit. This cost me £27 at a time when my earnings were only about £12 a week. It seemed extortionate, but over the years proved itself invaluable, keeping me warm and dry for many trips and adventures. The other thing I bought that day was a black silk balaclava for only £1 – again it was great as it kept my hair relatively tidy underneath my crash hat for many years. There were a few motorcycles for sale as well so we had a good look around before heading for home again.

Through the next couple of months all our thoughts were devoted to the route to take, settling for what looked like the most direct roads which took us through Peterborough and Leicester before joining the M6 which took us almost to Liverpool. I remember the approach into Liverpool, and seeing the Liver Birds building to find the docks as we had been advised, that was the easiest way to get where we needed. We arrived easily enough, all we had to do was to follow the trail of motorcycles all heading for the same place. Again, as we got near the ticket office, all we had to do was to copy the bikes ahead who obviously knew what they were doing. We pulled up at the top of the gangplank where the ticket office was signposted. Stu and Danny went down to get the boat tickets as Susan and I stayed beside the heavily laden bikes.

The boys came back about half an hour later, saying we had to now get in line for the ferry queue. The next procedure was to 'get your tanks empties here'. This was an archaic practice where all motorcycles had to have the fuel drained from the bikes before being allowed to embark. The reasoning for this was that it was a fire risk on board, they said that if you had too much fuel in the tank it could explode. (However, in hindsight it was proven that a full tank was less likely to be explosive as there was no air to ignite. This practice was kept going for years for whatever reason.) The worst of this was that if they took too much and you had a night boat, you could end up having to wait for a couple of hours to get fuel once on the island, so there were many disgruntled bikers not too happy about this. The only thing to do was to grin and bear it, as no-one was exempt and it was part and parcel of the 'rules' with no alternative. Anyway, we were resigned to this as we had been forewarned by some of our mates back home, so luckily we had not refuelled before embarking the way some people had been caught out. The question amongst most of us at that time was – where does all this petrol go? The general thought recognised by our peers at that time was it was given to the island taxi drivers, whether that was true or not I never found out. My belief is that the 'Steam Racket' company as it became known, probably owned the fuel garages near the terminal on the Island.

After having the lifeblood taken from our bikes, we were told to carry on down the slip road and join the back of the queue for the next available boat. We gaily followed the instructions and carried on down the road, around the corner for the back of the 'queue'. This was a sight to behold, the 'queue' was in the largest building I had ever been in. I guess it was an old ship's dry dock which did have a roof, but the 'queue' was enormous. The building housed thousands and thousands of bikes. Each line of the queue probably held about 100 bikes side by side and the lines of bikes stretched endlessly ahead of us, the building seemed to be about a mile long, packed wheel to wheel, panier to panier, full. The sight of all these bikes was absolutely awe-inspiring. It was larger than a football field, and absolutely astounding to us having come from a rural area, not used to seeing that many bikes all packed together so tightly.

This was probably the most tedious part of the trip as – five hours later – and counting, we were still waiting. There were so many boats which the Steam Packet company must have begged, stolen and borrowed for this massive annual event. I believe there were possibly eight or more ferry boats commandeered into practice for the four to six hour trip from Liverpool to Douglas. The timing differing between the different capabilities of the individual vessels, the calmness of the sea or not, and the time taken to load the varying capacities of ship. All these boats were in a continuous state of circular trips to and from the Isle of Man, as soon as it was unloaded, restocked and reloaded they were off again, taking perhaps an hour and a half for each reload. I believe we managed to catch the fourth or fifth boat circling the seas that day. The loading was a nightmare for our particular ferry, which was not designed for vehicles being a designated passenger ship. There was limited vehicular access, and the majority of motorcycles were then put aboard lining the various decks and gangways around the vessel. We had the frightening experience of seeing our bikes craned onto the ferry, horrifically chained in a trio slung underneath a dubious looking frame. Our bike was on the outside of the three, but all three were swinging about as they were craned onto the passenger deck, and manhandled into whatever space the crew hands deemed big enough; then were roughly tied in place with large sea-drenched hemp ropes to wherever there was a hook or railing to secure it. This was heart stopping to see our beloved motorbikes treated so abominably. But again, this was out of our hands if we wanted to get to the Island and all its promises.

Once aboard ship, the voyage seemed magical, the atmospheric feel leaving Liverpool for me personally as I watched the Liver Birds diminish into the distance was strangely soporific, I was not to understand why until years later; and that is too long a story to go into here. Needless to say, with the excitement we felt, we stayed on deck, keeping an eye on our bikes, but also enjoying the sea air. We found some space to sit and look out, the boys went to the cafeteria to get some food and drink for us to enjoy during the voyage. The seagulls had obviously got used to the tourists on these ferries and became so greedy, they resorted to almost feeding out of your hands as they flew around us throughout the journey. The ferry took about five hours before we got our first sight of the Isle of Man, but it did not take long to manoeuvre towards the Douglas Bay and we saw the beautiful seaside town for the first time. I had grown up in Brighton which had a great promenade and sea front, and this was reminiscent of that.

Chapter 15

ISLE OF MOTORBIKES (IOM)

I had never seen anything like the beauty I saw from the sea looking towards the shore, and it took my breath away as the sun shone on the long seafront and many buildings in Douglas; showcasing the long stretch of the bay. Both ends of the bay had large land masses, the southern end housing the dock, big enough to hold three large ferries at a time, although they had to sometimes tread water out on the sea to make sure the berthed ships were not about to leave harbour. If the way was clear, then they would approach and dock, allowing us hooligans to land and invade the very welcoming island for our fortnight of mayhem. The northern bank of the bay had a huge Victorian Hotel built on it, appropriately called the Douglas Bay Hotel and was majestic as it looked out over the sea and the bay. To me this was my idea of heaven, and hearing the motorbikes as they tore around the town, echoing through the streets, just blew me away.

We were quickly brought back to our senses as we then had the worry as our bikes were once again strapped to the framework to be craned off the boat, again looking very fragile as they swung against each other as they were lifted up and over the docksides.

We hurried off the boat ourselves, as quick as we could to catch up and claim our machines, Stu and Danny checking for any signs of damage or problems, but thankfully they were fine. We mounted the bikes and took off, ready to start our long awaited holiday to the full.

In a later trip, I did once see a horrifying spectacle as the bikes had not been clipped in properly and while two did somehow stay attached, they dangled precariously while the third one fell and promptly disappeared into the water. I really felt for the owner of that machine, as it not only lost him his bike, but must have ruined his holiday as he had no bike to ride around the island. I can only hope he was looked after both financially and ride wise, but I did not know the gentleman affected so never heard any outcome.

We were off – our first ride along the seafront, in the sun, taking in the sounds and sights to the full. The first thing that took me totally by surprise was the horse trams, and I was enthralled to see the noble horses trotting along the length of the seafront, pulling their trams behind them. It amazed me to see how they did not bat an ear or worry about the motorbikes buzzing around them, they were the most calm horses I had come across, and it was wonderful how tolerant they were. I know that if they had bolted, they could only go along the track that the tram was running along, but the fact they seemed totally unfazed was incredible. The many motorbikes riding in and around their lanes was never ending, and many bikes had quite loud pops and bangs as they were being ridden along the seafront, and the horses took it all in their gait. Humbling really, as this had to be learned, as we could not speak and tell them we meant them no harm. You wouldn't think that such gentle animals could co-exist so peacefully with the noisy, Castrol R smelling, weaving and bobbing race replicas which abounded over this two-week period, but they did.

The second thing which entranced me was to see an old-fashioned white hatted policeman in a traffic box, directing the many vehicles at the main junction about halfway along the seafront, at the bottom of Broadway as it left the confluence. I wondered what it must have felt like as the continuous stream of motorcycles rode at him, several would not have known he was going to be there. Was it frightening for him during his first few shifts to sit there waiting to be mown down by some erratic non-thinking riders or drivers. I must admit, I never heard of anyone actually running the officer down, and I know it would have been a short sharp punishment for any such misdemeanor, but it struck me as a fairly dangerous shift.

Stu and I had booked into a Bed & Breakfast on Broadway so we found our accommodation first. There had been an overbooking though, and our first three nights were spent sleeping down the road, but breakfast and evening meal in the booked premises until our proper room was ready for us. This was quite quirky having to walk up the road for sustenance. However, this was a minor inconvenience and soon remedied. Danny and Susan were a bit further away, at the Falcon Cliff Hotel just off Victoria Road. They were near the cliff lift which was still operating then, taking them down to the seafront or back, making it easy for us to walk along to meet them in the evenings. We settled into our B&Bs respectively, had a couple of hours for a much needed sleep catch up, and agreed to meet up later to then do our first 'lap' of the mountain circuit.

It is difficult to describe the effect of this hubbub of activity everywhere on this small compact island. Normally a peaceful and rural family island, long since a favourite holiday destination from the Victorian era, it was uplifting to see how the inhabitants coped with this huge influx of two-wheeled enthusiasts. From a general population of just under sixty thousand inhabitants, suddenly finding an influx of some 130,000 spectators. Add to the sheer numbers of happy bikers, the number of miles travelling each spectator would contribute, the island was cram packed to bursting. It was an often repeated phrase by the various traders on the island, that the TT funded the costs for the year, and the more genteel visitors for the rest of the holiday season would fund the profits. Of course, there is also the necessary thousands of extra staff needed, many youngsters from Liverpool and Ireland helping to bulge the walls and shops, it was a logistical nightmare. Talking to many of these TT workers, they were able to command good wages for this brief fortnight of absolute plenty. These extra workers manned everything from maids and cooks in the many hotels and B&Bs, the shops and many tourist areas, and not least the police were poached to swell numbers from the mainland, (aka 'abroad' in IOM speak). Add to that the burgeoning hospital in Douglas which was kept as fully staffed as possible, so many volunteer marshals and first aiders around the course during racing, all as essential as keeping everyone boarded and lodged, tented or whatever, I take my hat off to the organisers who do such an amazing job.

There was no room for another bike – anywhere – forget trying to park a car – most of the Manxmen's cars were stored out of Douglas during TT weeks. No point keeping them in town, if you moved it there would be nowhere to park when you return. Get stocks in before practice week and forget shopping unless you like to walk heavily laden down with goods; if you could get near the shops or sales counters. We found that if we had been out all day riding around and sightseeing or watching the practice sessions or racing, there was a general race to get back to your hotels etc with as much speed as possible. There were two reasons for this, the first because it was exhilarating to ride as fast as possible, emulating the racers who had just been past at phenomenal speeds, trying to copy and get the best 'racing lines' as we could, without becoming bonnet mascots for the oncoming traffic. There was no one way system operating in these early days, so it was a precarious time. There was an unofficial rule not to go the 'wrong' way when riding on the actual circuit roads. The second reason for this teatime haste was that if you did not get back quick enough, there would not be another inch of space to park your precious bike. The bikes were squeezed in, tail to the kerb, side by side, and it was often difficult to even stand your bike up to ride out of the line, without potentially scratching your fellow bikers prized steeds.

So many highlights over the holiday were enjoyed but one which we did several times over the week was our trips to the paddocks, to see Race Teams getting ready for the many sessions on the road. This was Stu's particular paradise as he could watch these engineers and mechanics break down and rebuild engines in a couple of hours, and offer the odd hand in times of dire need. The expertise of a confident tradesman is mesmerising for someone with a bent for their craft and it was sometimes difficult to drag him away. At least there were several trade and show stands to look at as well, so I was able to amuse myself, and I got to meet several of the big names as they drifted around the general scene. I even managed to catch a few words with the great Mike Hailwood who was a really lovely, friendly, down to earth chap. We often saw him about and he was always smiling. Charlie Williams was another favourite with the young women who were about, and Susan particularly had a bit of a crush on him. If we heard his name over the radio she would get all excited and cheer for him.

We did so many trips around the island, not just learning the track but we went everywhere we could.

For a change of scenery and to try and get away from the crowds we explored the northern tip and lighthouse in the St Andreas region, then back towards the circuit via Bride, this was a more empty area, but you still could not go anywhere without meeting and chatting with others of the same mind. On a few other occasions we went south towards Castletown, making sure we waved to the fairy's as we crossed over their little bridge. We found a lovely little café in Castletown, before heading off again to see Port Erin and then found the small road which took us past the chasms which we duly climbed all over, and managed not to fall down the many quite dangerous cracks and crevices in the rocks. It was quite unusual to be able to look down on the many seagull nests from above, and to watch the parent birds coming back and feeding their young. Just a short run further south and we came to the café and car park at the southern tip of the island – The Calf of Man – which was interesting as the tide was out and I thought we were going to walk across to the small peninsular, but we were advised not to as the tide would come in and we might make it over there, but then we would definitely be stranded as it was a particularly rough spot with many swirling sections of sea, not easy for a rescue attempt. Unfortunately we had to make the best of it, and went into the café for yet more tea and apple pie.

The next area we decided to take in was the western side with Peel Castle and the promenade featured on this day out. The beach was beautiful and sandy, but the water – ice cold; dipping our toes, we found out first foot (hand) how to turn our feet into blocks of ice. Lesson learned, we dressed and got back on the bikes and to the far side of the small harbour where the fishing boats came in. After admiring their boats and seeing their catches, we had a walk around the castle. It is awesome to walk around and feel the eons of time gone by, easy to imagine lives spent living in these ancient ruins. To almost feel the old horse and carts that would have brought wares and skills to the populace, bring life and perhaps itinerant entertainers to the realms. From here we travelled south again, having heard about the beautiful waterfall on this stretch of the island. Yay, another very welcoming café which fed us after we had walked down as far as the small craggy inlet at the bottom of this beautiful craggy valley – with its many waterfalls. I developed an incessant need to inspect and rate all the apple pies with cream that I could, but it was a hard job to differentiate. It meant I had to go back to several to ensure I remembered the tastes correctly.

After continuing down the western side and reaching Port Erin again, we returned back via some back roads and ended up coming out again at Braddan Bridge. As we were not going to return against the busy oncoming traffic we turned left and went around the circuit race way again, and this time we took a right hand turning to follow an interesting small road through Sulby Glen, another pit stop with obligatory apple pie, and then through some wild and woolly sheep country terminating back on the mountain road just past the Bungalow; we duly scuttled across the road to join in with the extremely quick traffic in order to ride back to Douglas for the evening. Even though it could be scary to jump into the bike stream at this point, the whole island was teeming with life. The following day we explored the eastern coastline from Douglas, finding yet another lovely inlet where we could scramble about on the rocks, a few intrepid fishermen were throwing handlines out and catching rock fish which resembled baby sharks. Susan and I were not so keen on these, and made sure we kept our fingers out of the way. Besides, they were slimy looking as far as I could see.

We continued on our way as we wanted to see the famous Laxey Wheel, which is the oldest and tallest water wheel you could imagine, and it was still operational, and of course, we had to inspect all the workings; climb to the top; clamber uphill to see the contributing cogs and wheels housed slightly upriver, before our menfolk were happy to move on. We crossed the hairpin to find the beach where to my delight, another café at the end of the small pebbled bit of shore. And I swear they cooked the all-round No 1 apple pie with fresh cream on the island, and by this time I had sampled all I could find so I feel qualified to judge. Second prize was the café halfway along the Sulby straight. Third prize to the small café nestled in the cosy cottages near the Snaefell railway terminal in Douglas, beside the stables. The fourth prize went to a little café in the main street from Parliament Square in Ramsey, heading towards the Ramsey Harbour, which I found during an interval in the racing whilst the roads were still closed. As there was also an interesting motorcycle shop close by, to keep Stu and Danny interested, Susan and I obviously had to test and approve the wares. Good job we were kept busy running, walking, scrambling up and down dale by the boys, or we might not have fitted our jeans and jackets for the road home. Just checking my thoughts; yes, just to confirm, the Laxey Beach café was the undoubted winner of Apple Pie and cream for 1975.

Sorry, I tarry from my story. We checked out the local railway station in Laxey, and bought tickets for the mountain trip: Thoroughly enjoying the panoramic views as we ascended back up the mountain to the Bungalow for a quick stop before continuing upwards to the top of Snaefell. Seeing the fantastic view on this beautiful day we were really lucky, although at the summit it was inevitably very windy. It proudly proclaimed on a sign board that you could see a view of seven kingdoms on a good day – Isle of Man, Scotland, England, Wales, Anglesey, Ireland, Northern Ireland. There was a signpost pointing to each of the seven kingdoms, so we could turn around and we did indeed manage to see them all; and yet again, I felt the atmosphere ancient peoples might have felt, as they stood and viewed the kingdoms from that point.

There are some intriguing traditions and folklore, including Tynwald, one of the oldest continuous parliaments in the world, purported to have been implemented over 1000 years ago, in a manner similar to the old Viking traditions brought over by the Danes and Norsemen ransacking the British Isles at that time. There are also many other tales abounding on the island, a quite mysterious one being 'how did the Manx cat lose its tail?' Many funny postcards showing the poor cat in various degrees of losing its rear appendage to being run over by motorcycle, car, horse tram or one of the various hobgoblin types who inhabited the many abundant and ancient groves. I guess that will be a tale that remains a secret, as cats can't talk and tell us, can they?

There are so many tracks dotted off the roads on the island, and in every little tunnel between the leafy glades there was yet another beauty spot, hamlet, nook and cranny. For an island so small, just over 30 miles long and about 15 miles wide it is unimaginable that so much could be squeezed into the space. There is something, or somewhere for everyone. Even if you are not motorcycle orientated, I challenge anyone to not find something that intrigues or inspires them, the pull of this island is beyond doubt, and with all the wonders of the world to see, I think this is one of Britain's best kept secrets. No wonder that so many bikers return year after year, sometimes going abroad to see other big motorcycle events, but to enjoy the Isle of motorbikes is the best!

Having ranted for the last few paragraphs, I will get back to the point of our holiday, and take you through some of my favourite viewing points we used around the circuit. I will give a brief summary of the aspects I liked, but of course, with 37.5 miles to choose from there is a place for everyone, and there are many extensive books on the differing sites. The ones I especially like are as follows:-

1 – The start line and pits are good, but very busy and noisy, but conveniences and food stalls a plenty. A short way on from here is Bray Hill where Agostini's famous wheelie photo was taken.

2 – Quarter bridge is quite spectacular and offers good photo opportunity as the bikes slow down and navigate the tricky double bends. Likewise, Braddan Bridge where the local church kindly put out viewing benches in their graveyard, and provide continuous food and drinks at their fundraising stalls, the church has probably re-roofed every church on the island by now. Both of these have outer access roads if you want to move between races during road closures.

3 – Greeba is quite popular, and the castle beside the course is nice to look at, but I have never been inspired to opt for this vantage point.

4 – The Highwayman Pub was a must stop and participate venue, although race viewing was not particularly great, as the car park was on the opposite side of the track to the sustenance. Great speeds obtained by all and sundry, this was probably where the cats lost their tails. However, there was a lovely Norton displayed in a glass case inside the pub which drew many an admirer.

5 – The next popular area to watch proceedings from was the corner at Ballacraine, which also happened to be another pub. Again, although the race machines had to slow down for this tight right-hander and was good for photos, there was limited viewing which quickly got crowded.

6 – To me, as I liked the peace and space between racing, there was the stretch called Barregarrow. Quite isolated as there was no provisions on site, you basically sat on a grassy wall having taken your own picnic and drinks, if you were canny enough to preplan. No facilities so not for a weak bladder, but the speeds of the competitors was phenomenal.

7 – Glen Helen – again a beautiful small rivulet on an outside stretch of the circuit. You are captured for the duration of racing, but the pub was really well set up for food and drinks, with several pathways to various banks for viewing. This shady glade is popular for a good reason. This bend means racers slow down for photos, great sustenance and viewing in the area.

8 – Kirk Michael – spectacular view of fast and furious racing within narrow confines of the main street, great pub on the right, but you are captured for the duration with no escape mid racing. If on the outside of the circuit, there are pathways where you could get back onto the Peel Road to change between races, if you had left your bike there beforehand.

9 – My next very popular spot is to see the bikes take off at Ballaugh Bridge, again gets very packed during

races, but we found it was hilarious to watch the tourists on their own vehicles getting the bridge all wrong and their ensuing antics trying to keep upright. (Usually heavily policed due to the crowds.) When we were there, the house beside the bridge let all and sundry trample their gardens while viewing the road and various jumps. You could not imagine the oldies back home being so accommodating, just wonderful, everywhere.

10 – The stretch from then on towards and through Sulby, Quarry bends and towards Ramsey were all fast and had their own attractions.

11 – Parliament Square in Ramsey – very popular and being in town, lots of pubs, cafes and take aways, facilities too of course. Good viewing, slower racing so good photo shots. Many streets leading up to the course offering accessible viewpoints, before leaving the town and heading out towards the hairpin.

12 – The hairpin, again, locked in during racing, so take your own picnic, but brilliant for photos. From a personal point of view, one of the most challenging points for learning your own 'race line' as it is extremely difficult to get around the hairpin on your own side of the road, hence nowadays this part of the circuit is one way only during TT period, for obvious reasons. Beware, some people forget this and inadvertently still try to ride upstream, forgetting that this is the last thing Salmon do in their lives. Many of these can be spotted as they often sport alternative number plates, often coloured ones.

13 – Leaving the hairpin are the twisty bends around Waterworks, which many walk down to from the next corner as there is more access to get away during road closures.

14 – Gooseneck – my all-time favourite spot. I just love sitting on the bank, listening to the bikes as they come up from Waterworks, looking down over the view to the pier at Ramsey. It was great to listen to the radio telling you who was in front, seeing if you could hear their approach, and perhaps know before the next radio point whether someone else had taken first position. The first person to come around may not be the first person in the race due to staggered start times, but this was also part of the fun, wondering right to the end, who had actually won. Remember to have a radio for this spot. It was lovely when the bikes came into view, and I spent a happy afternoon waiting and waving to Dave Croxford who appeared appreciative of my boob tube and hotpants as he came round, he was ever the flirt. I loved him, and to see him riding 'Slippery Sam' for what was to be its last race, was something I will never forget. Dave 'the rave' Croxford and Alex George shared this ride as it was a six lap marathon for the Senior this year, and they had an exciting battle with Helmut Dahn on his BMW. The Triumph won, not easily, but the BMW was ridden so hard that I believe he wore the top off his cylinders which protruded out sideways, and he had to retire near the end of the race. I was proud to see the British bike win, as the short circuits were filling up with foreign machines

and slowly were overtaking and eliminating our makes.

15 – From Gooseneck you could hear the bikes powering uphill and racing towards the Verandah, which was again not easy for spectating until they reached the topmost viewing arena on the circuit.

16 – The Bungalow – the highest point on the circuit, with a train line to catch you out if it rained. The motorcycle museum which was the original bungalow housed a good café, and between racing would get crowded with interested bikers looking and inspecting the yesteryear collection. Much fun had by all, looking, poking, prodding and discussing to their hearts content. Stu, Danny, Susan and I did the inevitable and decided to climb to the top of Snaefell from here, mid-racing, and watched the second race of that day from the top. It was funny to see the racing down below, but what a vantage spot, as we could see the bikes for a long way on their missions below. An extremely unique way to watch the racing.

17 – The mountain section here is very fast, whether racing or just enjoying one's own ride, and race week is full of opportunity to really see what your own bikes can do, or you can do to them. The bike will always come out on top as very few can really take a bike to its limits these days.

18 – There is a few miles of reasonable viewpoints from here on, but most are very windy and cut off,

but an experience all the same although no mid-race access.

19 – I always like the drop from Kate's Cottage down towards Creg ny baa, great spot, good mid-race access, car parking, pub and facilities. During our visit there was a footbridge over the track just downhill from the corner, and was interesting to watch from, especially the sidecar outfits. The outfit teams were to be especially revered, as their machines were definitely not the safest on the roads, due to the many undulations, lumps and bumps; the passengers must have been battered and bruised beyond belief. Courageous people, and for a long time the only way a woman was allowed to actually be in the racing, as chair person.

20 – Hillberry – fascinating to watch from here, pick your spot uphill from the bend, and wait for the excitement. Most 'newbies' will happily pick their spot, sit on the wall, be munching on their sarnies; anticipating the riders as they appear over the top of the hill – and the next thing the sarnie or drink goes overboard as the racers almost hit the spectator's feet with their helmets, sometimes less than an inch to spare. The second and third bikes through must laugh to themselves if they manage to see the bodies diving back and falling off the walls, I know I found it highly amusing to watch the carnage, and the shock on the faces of the un-initiated.

21 – The racing carries on down towards Sign Post, again interesting but not much room for viewing.

Also, being in Douglas again, those who did not come on their own transport could walk to this spot, so it can be crowded, but again good spot for photos if you can get in the right place at the right time.

22 – The tight bend around the Governor's bridge kink; again a good spot for a photo, but not easily accessed for viewing due to obvious dangers of the road at that point, many riders not quite making the bend, or forgetting altogether to take in that small hairpin and dip.

23 – Finally, back to the finish/start line. If you ever get to go, I hope you enjoy the island as much as I did!

Sitting there, watching the racing from wherever you choose, inspires one with an exaggerated sense of one's own abilities. One perspective to think about when riding the course was it doesn't matter how good you think you can ride, forget it, you will never be the best on those roads. Unless of course you are the best, as in Mike Hailwood, Mick Grant or Charlie Williams taking in the scenery for pleasure, or unscheduled circuit learning, a necessity as they have a 37.5 mile course to remember; with I don't know how many bends incorporating brick walls, hedges, bridges and long slopes leading to nice rock filled canyons. There will always be someone come up behind you, overtake and scare the life out of you, as they speed around at such a pace that you think you have got off your bike and were pushing it. That happened to us all, not just once but several times, and it is disconcerting when you thought you were all out, brains in pocket, and not to be messed with. The back pocket was also a bit close to your backside in moments of extreme pressure, but there is a perfectly good launderette in Douglas for untimely accidents not needing the A&E department. This island will sort the men and women from the superheroes, and leave you in no doubt about the prowess of those fearless competitors in their various races. Make no bones about it, the island will chew you up with ease.

The ultimate panic at the end of the holiday was the need to get home in a timely fashion as the inevitable time of our lives came to an end. In order to get home in time for work on Monday, we needed to go get a ferry for the Sunday. Ha ha, ho ho, it's not to work we go. The thought of that was bad enough, but to get a ferry home we had to present ourselves at the IOM Ferry offices at the terminal.

We queued on the Thursday to try and get a rough time schedule for our ferry home, but we did not have much say in what boats they allocated to us. We got a pass to say that we could start queuing for our passage from perhaps, 6am, 8am, 10am and so on for either the Friday, Saturday, Sunday or worse; any day the following week. Obviously there was a bit of panic as employers were not too flexible to workers saying we couldn't get home. This was not heard of then, and you could end up losing your job if you did not get home. The answer to this was to get the best you could, and then see if you could swap your passes with others in dire need, or able and willing to stay longer. Obviously there was the chance that you got home late and had to face the consequences. I remember queueing and swapping a couple of times, but eventually we managed to get Saturday afternoon passes, which meant we had to miss the last race, but this was a small price to pay, and we were relieved to be able to get home in time to have a bit of a rest before life brought us back to earth.

We decided to turn up a bit early at the dock to make sure that we did not miss the boat, and were pleased to be able to get on a proper vehicle ferry, so the worry of being craned on and off again was not there. That was a big relief as both Stu and Danny had been quite concerned if that scenario occurred again. In traditional IOM fashion, the boats were crammed full of bikes and riders, every available corner or cupboard filled with machinery or people. I am surprised they didn't dangle some of us over the side in hammocks, but perhaps they hadn't thought of that one. Anyhow, it was with a subdued and absolutely exhausted frame of mind that we left the island, we slept a bit on the boat as best we could as it was going to take a while to ride home. We docked at Liverpool about 4 o'clock and knowing it would take about five hours to get back, were hopeful we could do it before it got too dark.

We finally finished our adventure and culminated our holiday shortly after 9 o'clock that evening. Stu's mother was happy to see us and had a stew in the pot, waiting for our return. We were tired, hungry, but still fired up with all we had seen and done. The idea of a holiday being a bit of rest and relaxation was obviously not based on a biking holiday. After a cup of tea, and before we sat down to eat, we went outside to unload the bike and put it away in the garage. Stu had zeroed the trip on the speedometer before we left, only ten days beforehand, and he looked to see how many miles we had done. We were both astounded, to see that we had actually completed a total of **1,537 miles in ten days**, on an island no longer than 30 miles long and 15 miles wide.

What more can I say, but…

WOW! xxx

PS, it only took me 38 years to get this little gem out into the wide world, but I hope you like it. I will be getting the sequel out shortly, and possibly the prequel. If you would like more, please leave a review to encourage me.